Around
the GOLDEN RING
of Russia

Around the GOLDEN RING of Russia

AN ILLUSTRATED GUIDEBOOK

MOSCOW
PLANETA PUBLISHERS
1989

Written and compiled by
Yury Bychkov and Vladimir Desyatnikov

Translated by Alex Miller

Photographs by Vadim Tuzhikov,
also by Lev Veisman, Vadim Gippenreiter,
Vitaly Dorozhinsky, Yuri Mesnyankin, Lev Raskin,
Yevgeny Ryabov

ISBN 5-85250-191-3

INTRODUCTION

The beauty of the ancient towns, the imperishable value of their historical and architectural monuments, the gilded domes of the cathedrals, the autumnal gold of the forests and fields, the vital and inseverable ties linking the towns that grew up on the immemorially ancient routes to the north and south of Moscow—all these have given birth to a metaphor charged with meaning—the "Golden Ring". Here is the cradle of Russian culture. In these towns monuments of the 12th-17th centuries have been preserved to the present day: the ramparts, the fortress walls of ancient monasteries, whitestone churches, wooden buildings, frescoes, icons, brightly coloured majolica and wood-carvings.

The Golden Ring is also a popular tourist route. It runs through several regions in what is known as the Non-Black-Earth Zone.

The ancient towns of the Golden Ring are undergoing a period of intensive growth. Factories and research institutes are going up; pal-aces of culture and schools, higher educational establishments, technical schools, TV studios, printing works are in the course of construction, and tourist service centres are being created. Modern life proceeds at a dynamic pace filled with everyday worries and joys.

Among the other problems in this part of the country, particular concern is being shown to preserve the special character of the ancient towns on the Golden Ring. Just how much trouble is being taken to solve this task, which many other countries have in common, may be judged by accepting this book's invitation to visit the towns with the most monuments and museums along the thousand-kilometre route of the Golden Ring.

We have good reason for beginning our excursion at the walls of the Moscow Kremlin, since the capital and its ancient citadel are part of the Golden Ring. In the 12th and 13th centuries this town, founded by Yury Dolgoruky in 1147, was on the extreme edge of the Vladimir-Suzdal Principality. Moscow has performed the function of protector and gatherer of the Russian lands since the 14th century.

Each building in the Kremlin is a living witness of past centuries, a vivid page of history. Those massive walls can look back on devastating fires, outbursts of the people's wrath, and great revolutionary battles.

The Kremlin is the heart of this country, the symbol of its heroism and glory.

In March 1918, the young Soviet Republic's government, headed by Vladimir Ilyich Lenin, moved from Petrograd (now Leningrad) to Moscow. Over the Kremlin fluttered the red state flag of the Land of the Soviets. The Kremlin whose main towers are crowned with five-pointed ruby-red stars, is a symbol of peace, democracy and socialism.

Lenin, the founder of the Soviet state, loved the Moscow Kremlin. The austere, majestic beauty of the walls, towers, palaces and cathedrals made a profound impression on him. "We absolutely must preserve all relics of the past," he said to Bonch-Bruyevich, "not only as monuments of art, as is natural, but also as monuments of daily life in olden times. Excursions should come here, museums should be developed, and the historical background explained to visitors in detail." It was on Lenin's initiative that the Soviet government nationalized all art museums and issued decrees to protect our cultural heritage.

The chiming clock in the Kremlin's
Spasskaya Tower

Moscow, ancient and modern

The Kremlin Palace of Congresses

Red Square

The Lenin Mausoleum (built in 1930) stands by the Kremlin wall in Red Square. In the Upper Alexandrovsky Gardens the Flame of Eternal Glory burns on the Grave of the Unknown Soldier at the Kremlin wall. Massive blocks of dark-red porphyry contain soil from the hero-cities of Leningrad, Kiev, Minsk, Volgograd, Sevastopol, Odessa, Kerch, Novorossiisk, Tula and the Brest Hero-Fortress.

At the same time, the Kremlin today is still the living, throbbing heart of the country. It is here that the Soviet government works and that the elected representatives of the people assemble—the deputies of the Supreme Soviets of the USSR and of the Russian Federa-

Monument to Lenin in the Kremlin. 1967. Sculptor V. Pinchuk, architect S. Speransky

tion. The Kremlin Palace of Congresses is used for congresses of the Communist Party of the Soviet Union, and for many international congresses, conferences and symposiums.

Nearby, the vast city hums ceaselessly with its many millions of inhabitants. A huge industrial centre. A city of science and culture. A gigantic transport junction.

The Kremlin walls once marked Moscow's boundaries, then came the walls of the so-called White City—now the 9-kilometre-long Boulevard Ring, then the 16-kilometre-long Garden Ring. Moscow

Architectural monuments in the Moscow Kremlin

is now tightly girt by a Circular Motor Road, 109 kilometres in circumference. It is 40 kilometres from north to south and 30 kilometres from east to west.

The energy for its hundreds of up-to-date industrial plants is provided by electricity and gas. The natural forests and woods, the huge parks, boulevards and gardens give people shade in summer and a welcome refuge from the noise and bustle all the year round. During the 1980 Moscow Olympics hundreds of stadiums, palaces of sports and swimming-pools were in use.

Moscow has more than 30 permanent theatres, many concert halls, palaces of culture, cinemas, over 100 museums, thousands of architectural and sculptural monuments, memorials, and hundreds of research institutes and higher educational establishments.

Moscow is a clean, spacious city with broad thoroughfares and squares. Public transport is cheap, comfortable and reliable, and the Moscow Metro is, by universal acclaim, the most beautiful in the world.

In accordance with the General Plan adopted in 1971, Moscow is building intensively. The landscape is changing, and the city is acquiring new skylines, but there are no alterations to its radial-ring plan with the streets spreading outwards from the Kremlin.

We set out from Red Square and the Kremlin along a road which

The Bolshoi Theatre

Monument to the poet Alexander Pushkin.
1880. Sculptor A. Opekushin

Mir Avenue

is nearly a thousand years old. Here are hotels well known to foreign tourists—the *Moskva,* the *National* and the *Metropol.*

Sverdlov Square. Here is the world-famous Bolshoi Theatre and also the Maly Theatre. There is a granite monument to Karl Marx, and the bronze figure of Yakov Sverdlov, the first Chairman of the Central Executive Committee of the Russian Soviet Federative Socialist Republic.

We cross the Boulevard and the Garden rings and find ourselves on Mir Avenue. That was the name given in 1957 to the old Pervaya Meshchanskaya Street in honour of the World Festival of Youth and Students.

On Mir Avenue the attention is caught by the complex of monuments dedicated to the achievements of the Soviet Union in outer space. It includes Cosmonauts' Avenue with the monuments to Sergei Korolyov, the creator of the first Soviet cosmic systems that carried the first *sputnik* and the first spaceship with a cosmonaut on board into outer space. There are monuments to Gagarin, Tereshkova, Belyayev, Leonov, Komarov, and to Tsiolkovsky, the father of cosmonautics; there is also the impressive monument of sheet titanium to commemorate the conquest of space, with a Museum of Cosmonautics in the base.

A famous monument to the Soviet era overlooks Mir Avenue—a sculptural group, *The Worker and the Collective-Farm Girl,* by Vera Mukhina. This monument has been seen in France: executed in stainless steel, it crowned the Soviet Pavilion at the Paris World Fair in 1937.

The Worker and the Collective-Farm Girl is the monumental emblem of the USSR Economic Achievements Exhibition, which is visited by millions of Soviet people and hundreds of thousands of foreign visitors to Moscow. The ini-

Obelisk commemorating the conquest of space. 1964. Sculptor A. Faidysh, architects M. Barshch and A. Kolchin

tial letters of the exhibition, VDNKh, are common knowledge.

Near the road along which we set off on our journey stands one of the highest buildings in the world, the 536-metre 'needle' of the Ostankino TV Tower. Close by is the Ostankino Palace-Museum of Serf Art (17th-19th centuries) which has given its name to the All-Union TV Centre. Modern and ancient times are in close proximity here and make a striking contrast.

The first historical and artistic ensemble of great interest on our trip round the ancient towns of the Golden Ring is Zagorsk, an hour away by road.

The Worker and the Collective-Farm Girl.
1937. Sculptor V. Mukhina

USSR Economic Achievements
Exhibition

Zagorsk

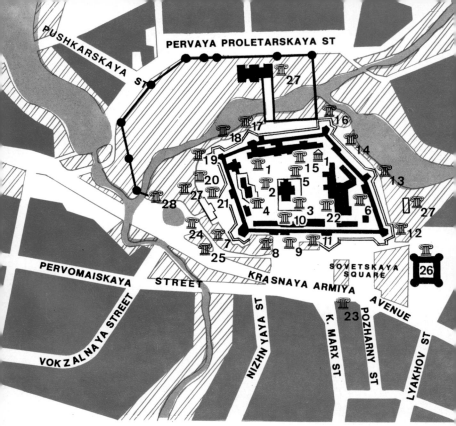

PUSHKARSKAYA ST

PERVAYA PROLETARSKAYA ST

27

17
18
16
14
19
13
20
1   15   1
27   2   5
28   21   3   6
4   10   22   27
24   11   12
7   8   9
25

PERVOMAISKAYA   STREET   KRASNAYA ARMIYA   SOVETSKAYA SQUARE
26

VOKZALNAYA STREET

NIZHNYAYA ST

K. MARX ST

23

POZHARNY ST

AVENUE

LYAKHOV ST

 Museums

1. The Zagorsk State History and
   Art Museum-Preserve (Trinity
   Monastery of St. Sergius)

 Historic architectural monuments

1. Cathedral of the Trinity
   (1422-3)
2. Church of the Holy Ghost (1476)
3. Cathedral of the Dormition
   (1559-85)
4. Refectory (1686-92)
5. Bell tower (1740-70)
6. Fortress walls (16th-18th cc.)
7. Pyatnitskaya Tower (1640)
8. Krasnaya Tower with gates
   (16th-17th cc.)
9. Uspensky Gates (mid-17th c.)
10. St. John the Baptist's Church-
    over-the-Gates (1693-9)
11. Sushilnaya Tower (16th-17th cc.)
12. Utichya Tower (17th c.)
13. Zvonkovaya Tower (16th-17th cc.)
14. Kalichya Tower with gates
    (18th c.)

15. Church of Our Lady of
    Smolensk (1745-53)
16. Plotnichya Tower (17th c.)
17. Kelarskaya Tower (1642-1849)
18. Pivnaya Tower (16th-17th cc.)
19. Vodyanaya Tower (17th c.)
20. Vodyanaya Tower Gates
    (16th-17th cc.)
21. Lukovaya Tower (16th-18th cc.)
22. *Chertogi* Palace (17th c.)

 **Historic and architectural
monuments outside the walls of
the museum-preserve**

23. Former monastery hostel (1861)
24. Church of the Presentation of the
    Mother of God (1547)
25. St. Parasceva Pyatnitsa's Church
    (1547)
26. Stable Yard (1790)
27. Civic building (19th c.)
28. Railing of the former
    monastery garden (19th c.)

Of Russia's small and ancient towns it would be hard to find one more famous than Zagorsk. Travellers are undoubtedly attracted mainly by the Trinity-St. Sergius Laura (Troitse-Sergiyeva Lavra), a historical and architectural ensemble of world importance. Many tourists coming to Zagorsk find within the walls of the Laura a unique, emphatically local museum which is nevertheless extremely well stocked with collections. It was founded during the first years of Soviet power in accordance with a decree by Lenin. The spacious museum has rooms devoted to ancient Russian painting, folk art, embroidery and jewellery.

We begin our tour of Zagorsk at the square in front of the Laura. Tourists' cars and coaches, kiosks and booths selling ice-cream and buns, the colourful dress of travellers from many countries and the black *klobuki* (tall hats) of the monks make a colourful spectacle. The square, like the Laura itself, is situated on a hilltop that gives a view of the ancient settlements graced here and there by the cupolas of churches and cathedrals, and of the road with its unending stream of traffic. As you stand on the square, you appreciate the size, impregnability and majestic beauty of the monastery's fortress walls. Every Russian monastery used to be built in this way primarily as a fortress.

Building work began on the walls in 1540 under Tsar Ivan the Terrible. Later they were raised to a height of 10-14 metres. They are three-tiered, with loopholes for cannon and small arms. The key defence points were the towers. Octagonal in plan, the corner towers—Pyatnitskaya, Vodyanaya, Plotnichya and Utichya—facing south-east, south-west, north-west and north-east respectively—were set well forward to give good fire-cover along the walls. The most beautiful is the Utichya (Duck) Tower. It is on the right if you stand facing the Main, or Holy, Gates. The tower received its name from the small stone duck surmounting the spire, made, according to the legend, to commemorate the hunting expeditions of Peter the Great who stayed at the Trinity Monastery of St. Sergius a number of times. The towers along the walls are flat and rectangular in

Zagorsk, old and new

24

plan. They are the Lukovaya on the south side, the Pivnaya and Kelarskaya on the west side, the Kalichya and Zvonkovaya on the north side, and the Sushilnaya and Krasnaya on the east side.

The tour of the monastery usually begins in the shade of the Main Gates, where wall paintings illustrate the life of Sergius Radonezhsky.

The Troitse-Sergiyev Monastery (Trinity Monastery of St. Sergius) came into being during a difficult period in Russian history. Ancient Russia was under the Tatar-Mongol yoke. Moscow and its great princes were uniting the forces of the people for the struggle with the conquerors and for the recovery of national in-

Old Zagorsk

The Utichya Tower. 17th c.

Walls and towers of the Trinity Monastery of St. Sergius. 16th-18th cc.

Church-over-the-Gates. 17th c.

26

dependence. Under these conditions Sergius Radonezhsky, a monk of outstanding intelligence and great spiritual strength, founded the Trinity Monastery in the 1340s. He immediately came forward as the active proponent of a united Russia. He propagated this idea through his pupils who in a short space of time founded 23 monasteries in North-East Russia. He pronounced anathema against the princes who opposed unification under the hand of Moscow. Sergius's authority was not to be

Fragment of the embroidered pall with a portrait of Sergius Radonezhsky. 1424

Cathedral of the Trinity. 1422-3

◀ *Vladimir Icon of the Mother of God.*
Late 14th-early 15th cc.

The Dormition of St. Anna. Pelena (cloth
placed under the chalice, etc). First half of
the 15th c.

contradicted. With his help the great Prince Dmitry Donskoi was able to muster under Moscow's banners the regiments of all the Russian lands and smash Khan Mamai's horde in 1380 at the famous Battle of Kulikovo.

A number of ancient portraits of Sergius Radonezhsky have come down to us: book miniatures, icons, frescoes and embroidered palls. The general consensus of opinion holds that the most authentic likeness is the one on the embroidered pall that originally covered Sergius's wooden coffin in the Trinity Cathedral. This remarkable work of Russian portrait embroidery is preserved in the Zagorsk Museum. It was executed at the beginning of the 15th century. There is no doubt

Those Standing at the Cross and Feasts.
Triptych. Carved by master Amvrosy. 1456

Detail of the architectural decorations on the Church of the Holy Ghost

Church of the Holy Ghost. 1476

that the design was supplied to the seamstresses by someone who knew Sergius extremely well. The portrait is impressive in its calm, its inner concentration and its strength of character.

The most remarkable work of art associated with Sergius is *The Holy Trinity* icon by his pupil and ward Andrei Rublev. Lenin referred to him as the first of the artists worthy to be commemorated. A bewitching power seems to emanate from this fine work. Peace and calm are radiated by the three inclined figures. The painter had the genius to express the predominant idea of his time—the call to peace. Since then five centuries have passed, but not a single line of the artist's appeal has lost its

Crucifixion. Relics cross. 14th-15th cc.

power. The works of Andrei Rublev have become world achievements of abiding importance to mankind.

As we continue our tour of the Trinity Monastery of St. Sergius, we gradually get to know the architecture, the interiors of the monastery cathedrals, and the exhibition in the Zagorsk History and Art Museum.

The present ensemble in the monastery comprises the white-stone Trinity Cathedral (1422-3) built over the grave of Sergius Radonezhsky; the Holy Ghost Church built by Pskov craftsmen (1476)—the monastery's first brick building and a masterpiece of ancient Russian architecture; the Cathedral of the Dormition

St. George and the Dragon. Slate icon in silver frame. Late 13th-early 14th cc.

(1559-85) decorated by Yaroslavl artists in 1684; the beautiful Hospital Wards built of red brick with elegant whitestone details, and the tent-roofed Church of SS Zosima and Savvaty (1635-8); the tsar's *Chertogi* Palace and the Refectory (1686-92) painted in chequerboard pattern with friezes of coloured relief tiles on the façades. The artistic image of the monastery is crowned by the many-storeyed bell tower (1740-70) built to the design of the brilliant Russian architect Dmitry Ukhtomsky. It is a graceful structure, 80 metres high, and surmounted by a dome in the shape of a crown. The twin columns, the rounded corners and the airy, open spaces of the tiers gradually diminishing in size towards the top give the tower an unusual lightness, a striving upwards. The bell tower, the focal point of an architectural complex that took centuries to form, gives finish to its outlines.

For many centuries the Moscow tsars and boyars considered it their duty to make valuable donations to the Trinity Monastery of St. Sergius. Thanks to these gifts and also to the industrial and economic activity of Russia's wealthiest monastery which owned many thousands of serfs, priceless art treasures were accumulated here. Everything that thrills us in the monastery—whether it be a monument of architecture, painting, sculpture or applied art—was created by the labour and skills of the Russian people. The Zagorsk Museum-Preserve houses one of the world's biggest collections of ancient Russian masterpieces. Works by outstanding painters, needlewomen and miniaturists, and also hundreds of unknown craftsmen are all worthily represented in the exhibition.

The icons by Andrei Rublev and Daniil Cherny on the iconostas in the monastery's Trinity Cathedral are national property

Cathedral of the Dormition. 1559-85

36

of world importance. They were painted in 1425-7.

Ancient Russian art, especially painting, has long absorbed the attention of many people. We know that Goethe was deeply interested in it and made it a subject of careful study. According to the famous French artist, Henri Matisse, who came to Moscow at the beginning of the 20th century, Russian art and his journey to Moscow in general gave him more than Italy. Studying the ancient Russian icons and discovering for himself their uncommon emotive, decorative and image possibilities—local colour and expressive outline—Matisse hit on a brilliant way of applying the methods of the ancient Russian masters to his own art.

Bell tower. 1740-70

A synthesis of form and content, an understanding of silhouette, line and especially colour—all were brought in the best examples of the ancient icons to a consummate perfection which will enthral the enlightened world for all time.

The icons and wall paintings in the Trinity and Dormition cathedrals and the other churches in the Trinity Monastery of St. Sergius are under the constant supervision of restoration experts. During the years of Soviet power these works have all without exception been cleaned of their centuries-old soot, and the paint layer has been reinforced. The restorers have literally given a second lease of life to a great many

Detail of the Hospital Wards porch. 17th c.

icons, since they had been over-painted many times during the centuries. The reason is that after about 80 years the linseed oil used to cover the icons was darkened by soot and grime, and the icon was renovated, that is, overpainted. Some icons had been subjected to this treatment five or six times. Soviet restoration experts were the first in the world to remove the paint layer by layer and transfer it to specially prepared new backings. A no less highly scientific method has been evolved for the restoration of frescoes, pictures, embroidery, silver and gold brocades, etc. For the examination and restoration of monuments of art the state annually allots the necessary funds for the use of the most advanced techniques, instruments and chemicals.

The chief organization of the Russian restoration experts is the Academician Grabar Research Centre, the head organization of Soviet restoration science. The centre is in Moscow, but its expeditions work everywhere. The specialists at the Grabar Centre have many thousands of artistic

Cup. 16th c.

Chalice (Communion Cup). First half of the 14th c.

Hospital Wards and the Church of SS Zosima and Savvaty. 17th c.

40

and cultural rescue operations to their credit.

In the Soviet Union the church is separate from the state. The Museum-Preserve and the Trinity Monastery of St. Sergius of the Russian Orthodox Church are situated on the grounds of the Laura. The monastery has extra-territorial rights. There are also the Theological Academy and the Seminary. The Patriarch of All Russia is the monastery's much-revered Father Superior.

We leave the ancient monastery

St. Ipatius icon. Cameo. 14th c.

walls. It is lunch-time. A new
restaurant, the *Zolotoye Koltso*
(Golden Ring), a conspicuous
building with its sumptuous décor
by Zagorsk artists, is now at the
service of tourists. It is a comfortable five-minutes walk away
across what is known as the
Podol—the low-lying ground
under the monastery walls.

Zagorsk is probably the most
popular town on the Golden Ring
route. From morning to night you
can see crowds of tourists on the
square in front of the monastery;

41

Chalice. English workmanship. 17th c.

42

impressions are exchanged, photos are taken, and souvenirs are bought at the *Beriozka* Shop which stands conveniently opposite the monastery gates. Peak hour begins towards lunch-time, when more and more coachloads of tourists arrive. However, it would be unfair to say that they are attracted solely by the monastery and the museum-preserve.

After seeing the golden-domed monastery and its beautiful museum for the first time, visitors begin to notice people of various ages with folios, clipboards or sometimes just sketch-pads in the streets, in the town squares, or in the picturesque corners of the park by the Kelarskiye Ponds. The local inhabitants walk by without taking

Dipper. 1428-36

Chalice. By master Ivan Fomin. 1449

Ancient Russian coins

The Trinity icon. By Andrei Rublev.
1420s

Frame of *The Trinity* icon. 16th-18th cc. ▶

any notice of them. An artist here is a common and everyday sight.

There is no town in the USSR where the profession of artist is as popular as in Zagorsk. There are often families of which all the members are artists—hereditary, what's more, and able to trace their origins back to the 17th century.

The craft of carving and painting wooden toys has long thrived here. There was also a papier-mâché toy industry in the 19th century. The humour of the people is noticeable in the cunning figures and in the portrayal of scenes from everyday life: an old man and an old woman quarrelling, or a *muzhik* dancing in a goat's head, or a merchants' tea party.

Chertogi Palace. Late 17th c.

Window frames of the *Chertogi* Palace

The famous Troitsky toys were sent to all the cities in Russia, and huge consignments were exported for foreign markets. The situation has not changed in our own times. The demand for toys from Zagorsk is high everywhere, and the arts industry is being developed further as a result. All the necessary conditions have been created for this purpose.

There is no regional town that can point to so many art-production and educational establishments and museums: two factories making elegant nested *Matryoshka* dolls and other colourful articles which will never gather dust on the shelves; Europe's, perhaps the world's, only Scientific Research Institute of Toys, with experimental production; a Museum of Toys, the Museum-Preserve in the monastery, a children's music and art school, a trades and technical arts college and the workshop of the local branch of the Artists' Union of the USSR. To this should be added the very ancient craft industries of the Bogorodskoye and Khotkovo bone- and wood-carvers with their workshops and training establishments.

The Refectory. 1686-92. *In the foreground*—St. Micah's Church. 1734

Mitre. 1626

Folk Art Section in the Zagorsk museum

Carved wooden toys from the village of
Bogorodskoye

Under Article 20 of the Constitution of the USSR, the state pursues the aim of giving citizens more and more real opportunities to apply their creative energies, abilities and talents, and to develop their personalities in every way. For the practical implementation of this article of the Fundamental Law, the state provides the necessary material conditions and gives every possible kind of support to creative workers. The best works, after being shown at republican and all-Union exhibitions, are bought by Union and Republican ministries of culture and by art commissions for museums and permanent mobile travelling exhibitions. In this way the meaning and essence of Article 27 of the Constitution is being implemented, which states that in the USSR development of the professional, amateur and folk arts is encouraged in every way. This article of the Constitution is particularly appreciated by the people of Zagorsk: there are hundreds of artists in the town—painters of nested dolls, potters, weavers, wood- and bonecarvers, craftsmen in other

Exhibits in the Zagorsk Toys Museum

Interior of the *Zolotoye Koltso* Restaurant
and Bar

folk industries, and also painters, graphic artists, sculptors, and monumentalists.

In the centre of Zagorsk, next to the monastery, is the biggest creative collective in the Moscow Region—the Zagorsk Art Production Workshop. Let us take a look inside. There is a special souvenirs section manufacturing figurines of fabulous *bogatyrs,* nested dolls, caskets, cups, powder boxes and bracelets. These goods are known all over the world and go to Britain, Japan, France, the USA, Brazil and the German Federal Republic.

Zagorsk is becoming a major tourist centre. The city is being improved and beautified. New housing estates and hotels are now in the course of construction.

Pereslavl-Zalessky

Monuments and places associated with military and revolutionary history

1. Lenin Monument
2. Yury Dolgoruky Monument
3. Alexander Nevsky Monument
4. Building used for sessions of the first Soviet of Soldiers' Deputies (April 1917)
5. Building used for sessions of the first Soviet of Workers' Deputies (April 1917)
6. Building in which Soviet power was proclaimed in the town (26 October 1917)
7. Ramparts of the Kremlin (12th c.)

Museums

1. History and Art Museum (Goritsky Monastery. 17th-18th cc.)

Historic architectural monuments

1. Cathedral of the Transfiguration of the Saviour (1152-7)
2. Church of St. Peter the Metropolitan (1585)
3. Church of the Forty Saints (1781)
4. Church of St. Alexander Nevsky (1778)
5. Church of St. Semion (1771)
6. St. Daniel's Monastery (16th-17th cc.)
7. St. Theodore's Monastery (16th-19th cc.)
8. Civic building (18th c.)
9. Arcade (*Gostiny Dvor*), early 19th c.

In the forests, near the road on the way to Pereslavl, there is a tent-roofed structure on pitcher-shaped columns and built of shaped bricks. This is the St. Theodore Shrine, or, as the people call it, the Shrine of the Cross. Tourists like to stop here for a breath of pine-scented air and to take snapshots as mementos. Indeed, this picturesque monument, which turns up so unexpectedly in the forest, puts the visitor in romantic mood and gives a foretaste of the town itself with its beautiful old buildings. As you enter Pereslavl, you have a charming view from the hill of the town comfortably spread out in the vale of Lake Pleshcheyevo which, on a bright, windy day, looks like a vast blue ploughed field. The old monasteries—of St. Theodore, Goritsky, St. Daniel and of St. Nicetas—stand like sentinels on the heights surrounding the ancient town of Pereslavl.

The tourist coach makes for the centre. Here, on Pereslavl's Krasnaya Square, stands a whitestone church as old as the town itself. It is best to begin one's tour here;

but first, a few words about the town's history.

Pereslavl-Zalessky is over eight centuries old. It was founded by Prince Yury Dolgoruky in 1152, five years after Moscow, on the *zalesskaya* (beyond the woods) side—hence the addition to the town's name, Zalessky.

The Russian appanage princes realized the importance of Pereslavl's geographical position and waged a long and bloody struggle for it. The chief rivals were Tver and Moscow. In 1302, Pereslavl permanently linked its fate with Moscow and in this way strengthened its position considerably in the struggle for the unification of feudal Russia.

Pereslavl was once rich and famous. It stood on the important Moscow-Arkhangelsk route along which trade was conducted with Western Europe in the 16th and 17th centuries.

In the 16th century, during the reign of Ivan the Terrible, Pereslavl became the bulwark of the *oprichnina* (bodyguard) which served as a weapon in the struggle with the boyar opposition. The tsar,

with the intention of transferring the capital from Moscow to Vologda, regarded Pereslavl as a strategic military point. An impregnable fortress, the St. Nicetas Monastery, was built in 1561-4 near the road to Yaroslavl and Vologda. You will see its mighty walls and magnificent cathedrals on your way out of Pereslavl.

The beginning of the 17th century brought much misery to the Russian people. Profiting by internal strife, the Polish-Lithuanian interventionists put Dmitry the Pretender on the Russian throne. He was really Grigory Otrepyev, a fugitive monk who passed himself off as the son of Ivan the Terrible. Civil war broke out. In 1608 the interventionists took Pereslavl. In

Cathedral of the Transfiguration of the Saviour. 1152-7

Detail of carved stonework

The East Entrance Gates of the Goritsky Monastery (17th c.)—entrance to the Pereslavl-Zalessky History and Art Museum

the following year an army commanded by Skopin-Shuisky, a talented military leader, drove them out of the city. The people of Pereslavl joined the militia under Minin and Pozharsky in 1612 and took part in the liberation of Moscow.

The end of the 17th century was marked for Pereslavl by an unprecedented burst of activity. In 1688 the young Tsar Peter the Great began building, for his military games on Lake Pleshcheyevo, the *poteshny* (amusement) boats and galleys which were the beginnings of the Russian Navy. From all over Russia came woodcutters, carpenters, smiths, and wood- and bone-carvers, all of whom had a marked influence on the develop-

ment of arts and crafts in the town. This is vividly confirmed by the collection in the Pereslavl History and Art Museum.

The story of how the 'small-scale' flotilla was built has not been lost. One of Peter's boats, the *Fortuna,* has been preserved to this day; you can see it in a branch of the local museum. The *'Botik'* Museum-Estate is situated on the south bank of Lake Pleshcheyevo, three kilometres from the town and not far from the village of Veskovo.

The ancient centre of Pereslavl is clearly marked out thanks to the earth ramparts which have been reduced by the passage of time but which are still high and stand there as witnesses to many centuries of

Carved wooden iconostas in the Cathedral of the Dormition, the Goritsky Monastery. 1759. Carved by Yakov Zhukov

View from the Goritsky Monastery

The Last Supper. Wood carving. Early 19th c.

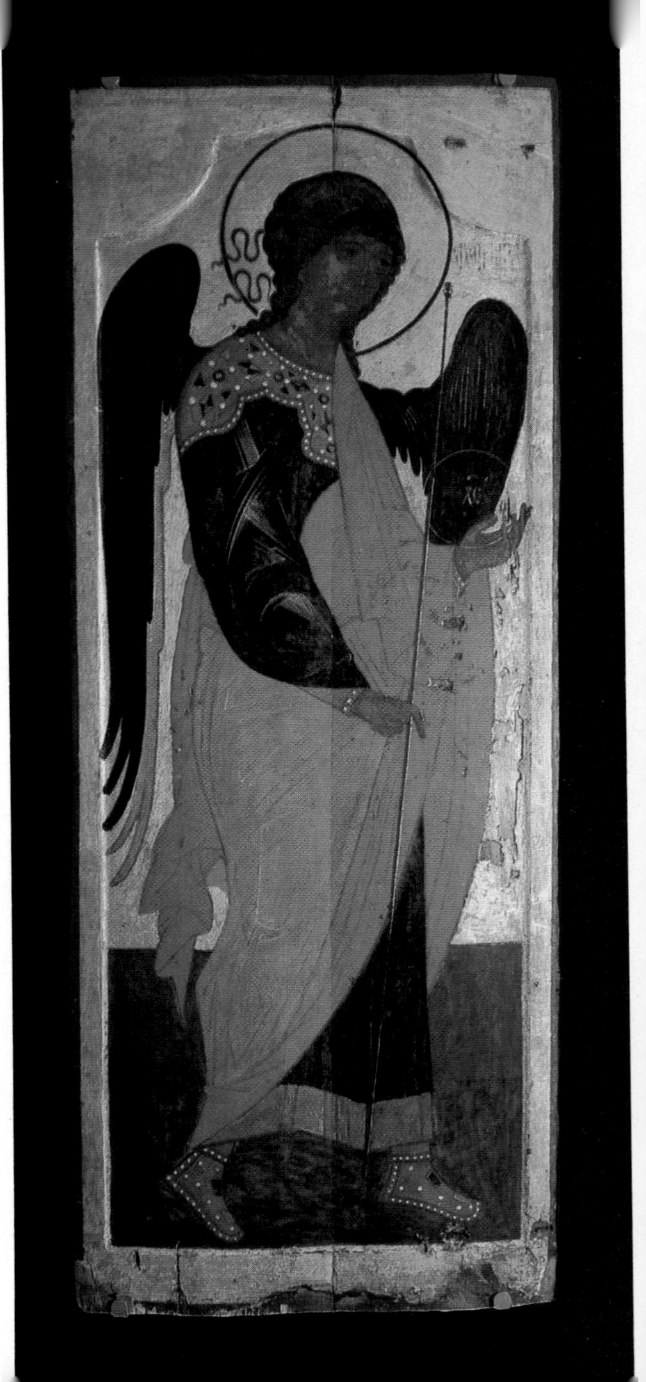

history. Only the capital city of Vladimir had even more impressive earth fortifications. Pereslavl's ramparts are two and a half kilometres long. The prince's palaces, churches, and the houses of the townsfolk were once inside the fortress. Time has obliterated all traces of them, and only Pereslavl's oldest building, the Transfiguration of the Saviour Cathedral (1152-7) gives some idea of how they used to build in Russia during the 12th century.

An early example of Vladimir-Suzdal architecture, the cathedral is far from graceful, but it has a power and force that bring down to us the harsh atmosphere that predominated in the times of Yury Dolgoruky. It is extremely plain

The Virgin and Child Enthroned icon. 16th-17th cc.

The Fall of Man icon, detail. From a church at the village of Pogost. 17th c.

and unpretentious. The grim walls with windows resembling the slits of fortress loopholes, the general squatness and the massive drum surmounted by a dome—all give the cathedral a monolithic, tough, burly appearance.

Pereslavl made a substantial contribution to the treasury of ancient Russian art. Two striking examples of the city's high cultural standards at the time of its foundation are the fragment of a 12th-century fresco from the Cathedral of the Transfiguration of the Saviour, depicting the head of an apostle (now in Moscow's State Museum of History), and Yury Dolgoruky's silver chalice which was sent to the Armoury in the Moscow Kremlin. A 14th-century icon, *The Transfi-*

guration, attributed to Theophanes the Greek, also comes from the Cathedral of the Transfiguration of the Saviour in Pereslavl and is now preserved in the Tretyakov Gallery.

A famous history of Ancient Russia, the *Summary of the Chronicler of Suzdal's Pereslavl,* which takes us to 1219, was written in Pereslavl, as was one version of *The Supplication of Daniil Zatochnik* (12th-13th cc.). Both these works are considered outstanding monuments of ancient Russian literature.

Prince Alexander Nevsky set out from the Pereslavl Citadel to do battle with the Swedes in the Neva Estuary in 1240 and with the knights of the German Teutonic

Order on Lake Chudskoye in 1242. The name of the unconquerable military leader of Ancient Russia has not been forgotten. The people of Pereslavl are proud of their fellow countryman. There is a monument to Alexander Nevsky on Krasnaya Square near the Cathedral of the Transfiguration of the Saviour.

Pereslavl is rich in monuments of the 16th-17th centuries. On Krasnaya Square tourists are sure to notice the elegant tent roof of the Church of St. Peter the Metropolitan built in 1585. The shape of

Gospel cover. Chased silver. 1693

Silver-embroidered banners. 16th c.

the roof was inherited by stone architecture from the Russian log-built churches which, like the beautiful fir-trees of the forests, soared over the vast open spaces of the Russian North. Stone tent-roofed churches are extremely rare. This principle lay behind the building of the world-famous Cathedral of St. Basil the Blessed in Moscow and the Church of the Ascension in Kolomenskoye.

In 1532 the Rostov architect Grigory Borisov was commissioned by Vasily III to commemorate the birth of a son, the future Tsar Ivan the Terrible, by building the Trinity Cathedral in the St. Daniel Monastery. The journey there from Krasnaya Square is of considerable interest for tourists. In the 17th

The St. Nicetas Monastery. 16th-19th cc.

century the cathedral was decorated by Kostroma's painters Gury Nikitin and Sila Savin, who were famous for their work in Moscow's Kremlin Palace and Armoury.

Among the architectural monuments in the St. Daniel Monastery of universal interest is the miniature All Saints' Church (1687), the Refectory of the Church of the Glorification of the Mother of God (1695), the block housing the monks' cells, the monastery wall and the magnificent tent-roofed bell tower built at the end of the 17th and the beginning of the 18th centuries. The big bell from the tower is now in the middle span of the Ivan the Great Bell Tower in the Moscow Kremlin. An inscription shows that it was cast in Pereslavl-Zalessky by the famous master craftsman Fyodor Matorin in 1678.

Pereslavl's architectural monuments are outstanding for the superior skills which went into them and which testify to the profound national traditions and high cultural standards among the local builders. These qualities were shown in the buildings of the Goritsky Monastery. Thanks to its location on the highest hill in the area, the monastery is visible from all directions. We approach it from the Moscow Highway. First come the Entrance, or Holy, Gates. We stop on the square in front of them to admire this pearl of Russian national art.

The gates and the walls of the

adjacent living quarters are richly decorated with patterns of shaped bricks and moulded ornaments. With a generous hand the anonymous architect decorated the walls with columned window frames and semicircles reminiscent of the *kokoshnik* (a traditional Russian women's head-dress), a fringe of beads coming down from under the cornices, moulded rings, and deep cavities. The gate arches are fantastically beautiful.

No ancient monuments have been preserved in the Goritsky Monastery. The present ensemble took shape in the 17th and 18th centuries, when the monastery's influence was spreading east and west of Pereslavl-Zalessky. The period of the monastery's pros-

Church of the Purification. 1778

78

Tent roof of the bell tower of the
Cathedral of the Trinity in the St. Daniel
Monastery. 1689

Plaque in the wall of All Saints' Church
in the St. Daniel Monastery. 1689

The St. Daniel Monastery. 16th-17th cc.

81

Rampart in Pereslavl-Zalessky. 12th c.

Tent-roofed Church of St. Peter the Metropolitan. 1585. Bell tower erected in the second half of the 19th c.

perity, when the bishop's residence was situated within its walls, is illustrated most vividly by the Cathedral of the Dormition built in the 1750s. It can hardly be equalled anywhere in Russia for size, elegance of interior decoration or, above all, for its acoustics, which are truly amazing.

The former Goritsky Monastery now accommodates the Pereslavl History and Art Museum. It was founded in the first years of Soviet power. In variety and size of stocks it is one of the biggest regional museums in the USSR with a collection that includes tens of thousands of exhibits, a library of thirty thousand books, extremely rare inscriptions and messages, old printed books, and editions published in the lifetime of leading Russian writers of the 18th and 19th centuries, Kantemir, Derzhavin, Karamzin and Pushkin.

Of the forty-seven rooms in the Pereslavl Museum nearly half are used for the art gallery. Artists represented here include Shishkin, Makovsky, Polenov, Malyavin, Kasatkin, Benois, Lanseré, Serebryakova, Korovin, Yuon—all familiar to us from Moscow's Tretyakov Gallery collection which covers the whole of Russian art.

Even the biggest museums might well envy Pereslavl's ancient Russian art collection. There are true masterpieces there, such as *The Archangel Gabriel* and *The Archangel Michael* icons (16th century) from the St. Nicetas Monastery; *SS Peter and Paul* (15th century) and *The Fiery Ascension of Elijah the Prophet* (16th century) from the Church of the Intercession; *The Dormition of the Mother of God* (16th century) from the Dormition Cathedral in the Goritsky Monastery. Judging by the first-class local paintings, it can be assumed that the town had its own famous master craftsmen in the past. The names of the Pereslavl painters, Nikifor Andreyev and Grigory Nikitin, have come down to us on a signed icon, *St. Nicholas the Miracle-Worker* (mid-17th century), from the Church of St. Barbara. Icons were not usually signed in ancient times, and establishing the painter's name is consequently a labour consuming task for the experts.

82

Peter the Great. Bronze sculpture. 19th c.

Lake Pleshcheyevo

The Pereslavl wood-carvers were not inferior to the painters. In 1867, at the World Exhibition in Paris, the 17th-century carved Tsar Gates from the Church of the Presentation in the Rybachya Sloboda were awarded a big gold medal and a diploma.

It was only at the beginning of the 20th century that the experts began to take an interest in wooden statuary. In pre-revolutionary museum exhibitions works by masters of this art form had a very modest place. In Soviet times interest in what was truly an art of the people grew considerably. This was largely facilitated by the publication of a series of scientific works by such well-known scholars as Mikhail Alpatov, Victor Vasi-

Monument to Peter the Great in the *Botik* Museum-Estate. 1852. Architect A. Campioni

The *Botik* Museum-Estate

lenko and Nikolai Pomerantsev, by the holding in Moscow of big exhibitions of wooden sculpture, and by the inclusion of work by folk wood-carvers in the museum exhibitions on the Golden Ring.

There is a collection of over a hundred sculptures in the Pereslavl Museum. The most outstanding is *The Saviour Grieving at Midnight* (17th century) from the Cathedral of the Dormition and no museum in Russia has anything comparable. As in every major work of art, there is a great deal implied in the carving, which makes this sculpture a masterpiece with as much depth and range in the feeling it conveys as any of the best icons by Rublev and Dionysius.

Russian embroidery is rightly called 'painting with a needle'. The profound sense of tradition and kinship with the people, the innate good taste and skill of the needlewomen are the reasons for the rare achievements of the embroideresses of Ancient Russia. There are many interesting works by Russian embroideresses in the Pereslavl museum.

The museum is an important educational and cultural feature of Pereslavl. It not only forms the aesthetic tastes of the visitors with its beautiful examples of art in all its aspects. It instils a sense of continuity, civic commitment and respect for the heroic and hard-working past. The monuments of the revolutionary movement and of the period when Soviet power

The Trubezh River

was being established, the museum's impressive section covering the Great Patriotic War, and life and work in the modern town—all are widely represented in the exhibition.

In 1969, on the eve of the 100th anniversary of Lenin's birth celebrated in 1970, a new branch of the Pereslavl Museum was opened at Gorki, once the estate of the Ganshins. It was here, in July and August 1894, that an illegal book by Lenin, *What the "Friends of the People" Are and How They Fight the Social-Democrats* was printed. Unfortunately, the Ganshins' house was destroyed by fire in 1927, and also part of the park and the neighbouring buildings. The museum-

Interior of the *Skazka* Restaurant

The *Skazka* Restaurant

estate has been restored and now looks as it did when Lenin saw it on his arrival in 1894.

For forty years the Pereslavl Museum was under the directorship of Merited Cultural Worker of the RSFSR, Konstantin Ivanov who comes from a background of textile workers. He has written books, tourist guides, and pamphlets about the museum and about the town's monuments. He has inspired in the inhabitants of Pereslavl-Zalessky a devoted love for the museum. It was on his initiative that 'Museum Day' was inaugurated in the town in 1934. Since then, annually on 2 May, almost the whole town goes to the Goritsky Monastery. Many also come from the neighbouring villages. This has already become a fine tradition and a local festival.

Today's Pereslavl, although many big industrial plants are operating and new housing estates are going up in this regional centre, is still a protected area. The town enchants everyone who arrives here with its particular cosiness, its calm, its well-kept narrow streets, the clean flow of the Trubezh, the upturned boats along the banks of the river. And how beautiful is the vast Lake Pleshcheyevo! It is not surprising that Pereslavl and its environs were a favourite place of rest and work for many Russian writers, artists and performers, including Fyodor Chaliapine, Konstantin Korovin and Mikhail Prishvin.

In recent years, as a result of the rapid development of tourism, Pereslavl is becoming one of the most attractive places on the Golden Ring.

You always come to this town with pleasure and leave with regret.

Rostov
Veliky

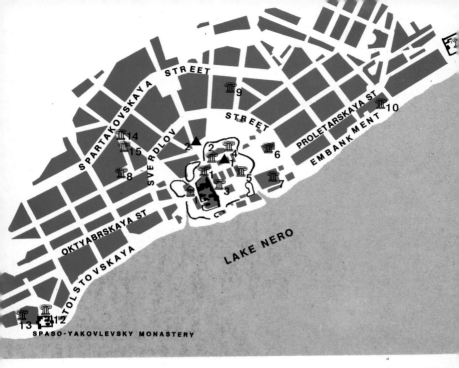

SPASO-YAKOVLEVSKY MONASTERY

▲ **Monuments and places associated with revolutionary and military history**

    1. Building in which Soviet power was proclaimed in the town (18 December 1917)
    2. Ramparts (1630s)

🏛 **Museums**

    1. Rostov and Yaroslavl Museum-Preserve of Art and Architecture (the Kremlin; Metropolitan's Courtyard, 17th c.)

🏛 **Historic architectural monuments**

    1. Cathedral of the Dormition (16th c.) with bell tower (17th c.)
    2. Church of the Saviour-on-the-Market Place (*Spas-na-Torgu*), 1685-90
    3. Arcade (*Gostiny Dvor*), 1830

    4. Church of St. Isidore the Blessed (Church of the Ascension), 1566
    5. Church of the Nativity (17th-18th cc.)
    6. Tax Yard (*Mytny Dvor*), 1830
    7. Railings of the town garden (1830)
    8. Church in Tolga (1761)
    9. Church of St. Nicholas-on-the-Vspolye (1813)
    10. Church of SS Cosma and Damian (1775)
    11. St. Avraamy's Monastery (16th-17th cc.)
    12. St. Jacob's Monastery of Our Saviour (17th-19th cc.)
    13. Church of the Saviour-on-the-Sands (*Spas-na-Peskakh*), 16th-17th cc.
    14-15. Civic buildings (18th c.)

On the way to Moscow, not far from Rostov, a plain begins, undulating here and there, with woods and open fields. Climbing from hill to hill, the road takes us to the edge of the Lake Nero Depression and runs along its west shore for a few more kilometres. As we draw nearer to ancient Rostov, the gilded domes of the churches and the white fortress walls of the majestic Kremlin shine more and more vividly in the sun.

Russian master craftsmen put inexhaustible fantasy and skill into every one of the Rostov Kremlin buildings, be it the mighty citadel walls with their eleven towers, the spacious limestone palaces or the church interiors with their fantastic wall frescoes. As soon as it was built in the 17th century, the Rostov Kremlin became one of the great sights of Russia. To this day it thrills us with its unique beauty, wealth of architectural forms and variety of the gilded domes.

In plan, the Rostov Kremlin is an irregular rectangle and covers an area of about two hectares. Unlike most Russian kremlins and monasteries, it does not have a monumental cathedral to dominate the rest of the buildings. The centrepiece of the ensemble is a spacious courtyard with buildings of about the same size, grouped along the walls. The town's main cathedral, the Cathedral of the Dormition, is outside the Kremlin walls. It is adjacent to the Kremlin, but still stands separately as part of a self-contained civic ensemble with the Shopping Centre (*Torgovyie Ryady*), bell tower, and the Church of the Saviour-on-the-Market Place (*Spas-na-Torgu*).

It is with the Cathedral of the Dormition that we begin our tour of Rostov. Massive and majestic, it was put up on the site of 12th- and 13th-century buildings during the reign of Ivan the Terrible. At this time Rostov played a significant part in the life of the Russian state. It was a major trading centre on the road from Moscow to the White Sea. All the big expeditions of Russian pioneers leaving to tame the northern and eastern wilds passed through Rostov in the 16th and 17th centuries.

94

Part of a bell in the Rostov bell cote

Stone window frame

Detail of stone decorations

Gate grille, the Cathedral of the Dormition

Lion-mask handle on the ancient doors of
the Cathedral of the Dormition. 12th c.

The Cathedral of the Dormition has the five domes traditional in Ancient Russia. The interior walls are decorated with paintings. A shining example of the applied art of that time is to be seen on the west cathedral doors which are decorated with iron handles in the form of lion masks (12th century).

The Cathedral of the Dormition, as the tourist will notice when he enters the city from the direction of Moscow, is not separate from the Kremlin visually, but is closely connected with its walls and towers. Credit is due for this to the Metropolitan Iona Sysoyevich. He was responsible for the general design of the whole group and for helping to create and work

Ancient weather vanes

Walls and towers of the Rostov Kremlin

South-west tower and the Church of
St. Gregory the Divine. 17th c.

Panorama of Rostov Veliky

Top of a Kremlin tower

Red (Krasnaya) Chamber. 1670-80

out the style of a number of Kremlin buildings which have a deservedly prominent place among the architectural complexes of Ancient Russia.

The Kremlin walls and towers were built in 1670-5. The walls are relatively thin, the towers and gates are richly decorated, while the loopholes and battlements are ornamental rather than functional. The gate churches are directly incorporated into the composition of the walls: the Church of the Resurrection on the north wall, built in 1670, and the Church of St. John the Divine on the west wall, built in 1683. Both churches stand over the Entrance Gates, and each is supported on two sides by graceful round towers.

The five-domed Church of the Resurrection stands over the Holy Gates, so called because the ceremonial processions of the Metropolitan to the Cathedral of the Dormition used to pass through them. The gates are richly decorated. The church gallery and its walls are thickly covered with paintings of rare beauty, which were applied *al fresco*, that is, on the damp plaster, a technique demanding great skill, fine draughtsmanship and accurate choice of colours.

The Church of St. John the Divine is similar to the Church of the Resurrection, except that the interior space tends vertically upwards in a more pronounced manner. The church walls are painted with scenes from the life of St. John the Divine and St. Avraamy of Rostov, the legendary Christian missionary in Rostov.

The most important group of buildings is in the south-east part of the Kremlin and includes the civic buildings which went up in 1672-80, and the true gem of the Kremlin complex, the Church of the Saviour-in-the-Vestibule (*Spas-na-Senyakh*), 1675. The cube-shaped church with its modest architectural design has a single

Cathedral of the Dormition. 16th c.

vault and is crowned with a small dome. The interior has no equivalent in Russian architecture. Half of the interior is taken up by a high raised *soleya* (elevated floor in front of the altar), decorated with a stone arcade resting on thick gilded columns. The arcade of the *soleya* is joined by the arches to the stone iconostas. All the walls, the iconostas, and the arcade of the *soleya* are decorated with frescoes executed in the 17th century by Timofei Yarets, a native of Rostov, Dmitry Stepanov from Vologda, and Ivan and Fyodor Karpov, natives of Yaroslavl.

Three hundred years have passed, and the Rostov frescoes have not lost their artistic merits. They are a delight to the eye thanks

Bell cote in the Rostov Kremlin. 17th c.

to the harmonious combination of soft turquoise and pale-blue shades with golden ochre, rose and white. The subjects are treated with freshness, originality, and with the tendency towards the secularization of ancient Russian painting, which was becoming more and more influenced by the everyday life, rituals and customs of the people. If one looks closely at the Rostov frescoes, it is not hard to detect behind the religious subjects the real life and, what is more, very profound real-life content. When creating their works, the artists of Ancient Russia were inspired by the images of the Russian people, their own contemporaries—tillers of the soil, tradesmen, soldiers. The Rostov

103

Church of the Saviour-in-the-Vestibule (*Spas-na-Senyakh*). View from north-east. 1675

frescoes leave us in no doubt of this.

When viewing the Rostov Kremlin, it is possible, without descending to ground level, to walk round the walls and not only visit all the churches, but to see all the other buildings as well—Chambers for Church Dignitaries, the Prince's Chambers, the White Chamber, the *Otdatochnaya* Hall where people came to pay their respects, and the Metropolitan's House, all of which now accommodate a museum exhibition.

The Rostov Museum is famous for its collection of enamels, ancient icons, copper castings, coins, wooden sculptures and folk carvings. Every section in the mu-

Church of St. John the Divine. 1683

SS John and Prokhor Sailing to the Isle of Patmos. Fresco. 1683

seum can claim at least one masterpiece.

The production of enamels in Rostov has ancient and solid traditions. Particularly valuable are the Rostov enamels of the end of the 18th and the beginning of the 19th century; they are exceptional for clarity of outline and rich variety of colour. In our own times the traditions are being kept up by the magnificent enamellers at the *Rostovskaya Finift* Factory. The museum exhibition has on display examples of the 18th and 19th centuries and also the best work by contemporary enamellers.

The Rostov craftsmen formerly made miniature enamelled icons, decorations for church books and for the robes of the higher clergy.

Gallery of the Church of the Resurrection. 17th c.

Stone patterns on the Church of the Resurrection.

Frescoes in the Church of the Resurrection.
Circa 1670

Pilate Washes His Hands. Fresco in the
Church of the Resurrection

Since the end of the 19th century the artists have concentrated more and more on orders of a secular nature. Today's craftsmen in Rostov specialize in souvenirs, elegant women's ornaments, plaquettes with architectural views and miniature paintings with Russian songs and fairy-tales as their subject.

The museum exhibition vividly demonstrates that the Rostov enamellers knew the work of their Limoges and English counterparts. There are no direct borrowings, but studying the experience of the foreign craftsmen played a definite part in widening the technical resources of the Rostov artists.

The single-columned White (Belaya) Chamber. 1675

The Archangel Michael icon. 14th-15th cc.

114

Portrait of the Metropolitan Iona
Sysoyevich, builder of the Rostov Kremlin.
Late 17th c.

St. George the Victorious. Wooden
sculpture. 15th c.

To enumerate the exhibits in the Rostov museum, even if we confined ourselves to those of the very highest artistic quality, would be impossible in a brief article. We would nevertheless like to mention such masterpieces as *The Archangel Michael* icon (14th-15th cc.), the carved limestone cross from the grave of the son of Stefan Borodaty, the prince's scribe (1458), and the wooden figure, *St. George the Victorious* (15th century), carved by the outstanding Russian architect, builder and sculptor Vasily Yermolin.

Among the many buildings in the Kremlin, one that invariably attracts attention is the mighty four-tiered bell tower built in 1682-7. Even from a considerable distance it is possible to see in its spans the great bells on which the Rostov chimes are played.

Since ancient times the chiming of bells has accompanied the life of the people, calling them to battle, sounding fire alarms, summoning congregations, or joyfully greeting heroes returning from the battlefield. Novgorod the Great, Pskov, and Moscow were famed for their bells since olden times, but there was never anything anywhere to match the Rostov chimes.

There are thirteen bells in the bell tower of Rostov's Cathedral of the Dormition. The ringers stand so that they can see one another and keep in time. A joyful major chord is characteristic of the Rostov chimes which can be heard some twenty kilometres away.

It seems only right to begin the tour of Rostov with a visit to the museum and the Kremlin monuments. The town is a true preserve of 17th-century architecture. But this is only a part of what is to be seen there.

Rostov in winter

To the north-east of the Kremlin, near the ramparts, stands the small and beautiful one-domed Church of St. Isidore the Blessed. It was built by Moscow master builder Andrei Maloi in 1566, and its shape is typical of Moscow architecture at that time.

Also by Andrei Maloi is the great Cathedral of the Epiphany (1553) of the St. Avraamy Monastery on the east fringe of the town, one of the oldest surviving architectural monuments in Rostov.

The St. Jacob Monastery is situated on the west fringe of the town, on the shore of the lake. Within the stone wall and towers stands the Church of the Conception, built at the time of the Metropolitan Iona Sysoyevich in 1686, and the Church of St. Demetrius, an outstanding monument in the Russian neo-classical style. It was built in 1794-1801 by Dushkin and Mironov, two serf architects who belonged to Count Sheremetev.

In the 18th and 19th centuries Rostov was a trading town known in Russia and abroad as a market-gardening centre. In the last quarter

Products of the *Rostovskaya Finift* Factory

Restorer at work

Entrance to the *Krasnaya Palata* Hotel
Shopping Centre (*Torgovyie Ryady*). 19th c.

Guests in Rostov

Railway terminal

of the 19th century industry appeared in the form of a flax mill, a coffee and chicory works, and a molasses factory.

Nowadays, Rostov is seen primarily as a unique historical and architectural complex and a city-preserve. It is not being developed as an industrial centre, and no large-scale construction work is in progress. Each new building project in Rostov is carried out with a view to the location of the architectural monuments.

Rostov is a district centre of the Yaroslavl Region, and it proudly calls itself Rostov Veliky (the Great). The magnificent and lovingly preserved old buildings, the paintings and the famous Rostov chimes are the pride and glory of Russian art.

Yaroslavl

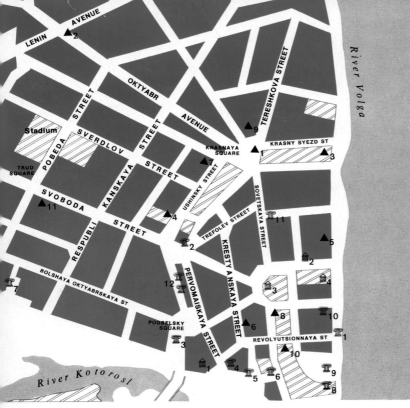

▲ **Monuments and places associated with revolutionary and military history**

1. Lenin Monument
2. Karl Marx Monument
3. Nikolai Nekrasov Monument
4. Fyodor Volkov Monument
5. Room used for secret meetings by the Yaroslavl Committee of the RSDLP (1906-7)
6. Building used by the Soviet of Workers' Deputies (1917)
7. Building which housed the City Headquarters of the Red Guards in 1917
8. Memorial *To the Fighters for the Revolution*
9. The house used by the Headquarters of the Northern Front (1918-9)
10. Monument in honour of the battle and labour exploits of the people of Yaroslavl during the Great Patriotic War of 1941-45
11. Obelisk in honour of the 30th Anniversary of Victory

🏛 **Museums**

1. State History and Architecture Museum-Preserve—Our Saviour Monastery, 13th-16th cc.
2. Branch of the History and Architecture Museum-Preserve—Church of St. Nicholas Nadeyin (1620-2)
3. Branch of the History and Architecture Museum-Preserve—Church of St. Elijah the Prophet (1647-50)
4. State Art Museum

🏛 **Historic architectural monuments**

1. Volzhskaya Tower (1658-68)
2. Znamenskaya Tower (1660-2)
3-7. Architectural monuments (second half of the 17th c.)
8. Metropolitan's Chambers (17th c.)
9. Architectural monument (church, 1825-31)
10. House of the former Society of Physicians (late 18th c.-early 19th c.)
11. Architectural monument (church, 1644)
12. Rotunda and part of the former Arcade (1813-18)

From early spring right into the depths of autumn, Russia's main 'street', the Volga, is very busy. From Yaroslavl, a big industrial and cultural centre on the Upper Volga, self-propelled barges head up and down the river loaded with car tyres, diesel engines, machine tools and synthetic rubber. The city manufactures a variety of products and sends them all over the country, but car tyres and diesel engines are the main contribution to the common 'kitty' of the Soviet Union's general output.

The city has great labour traditions. Here, in Yaroslavl, the first Soviet heavy automobile was assembled back in 1925. Later, the first Soviet tip-up lorry was made, as were the first trolleybus, the first Soviet diesel engine, and the world's first artificial rubber car tyre. On August 1985 by a decree of the Presidium of the Supreme Soviet of the USSR, timed to coincide with the 975th anniversary of the city, Yaroslavl was awarded the Order of the October Revolution.

In order to see for yourself the monuments of Yaroslavl's nine hundred years of history and to learn about the traditions of remote antiquity, walk along the Volzhskaya Embankment from the monument to the poet Nikolai Nekrasov as far as the Strelka, the spot where the river Kotorosl flows into the Volga. It is here that Yaroslavl's recorded history began. In 1010 Rostov Prince Yaroslav the Wise founded a town here and gave it 'his own name'. The prince thus gained control of the entire waterway from Rostov to the Volga across Lake Nero and along the Kotorosl that flows from the lake.

Not far from the Strelka stands the majestic ensemble of the former Transfiguration of the Saviour (Spaso-Preobrazhensky) Monastery. The mighty walls with their defence towers enclose a large area in which there is ample space for the cathedral, the churches, the *terems* and the chambers. It is now the site of the State History and Architecture Museum-Preserve, the biggest in Yaroslavl. Before entering the museum rooms, note the Transfiguration of the Saviour Cathedral, Yaroslavl's oldest, built in the 16th century. The cathedral is easily distinguished from the other buildings by its gilded

central dome. As Soviet archaeological excavations have shown, it was built on the site of an even older cathedral which was destroyed by fire in 1501 and which, in the 13th century, was one of the most revered and wealthy churches in the Rostov-Yaroslavl lands.

The sacristy of the Transfiguration of the Saviour Monastery was continually replenished by rich donations from the princes and the boyars. There were thousands of rare books, presentation letters, and manuscripts in the monastery library, with over a thousand volumes of Greek manuscript books alone. At the end of the 18th century an ancient copy of *The Lay of Igor's Host,* a 12th-century Russian literary work of genius, was found in the monastery library. *The Lay* is on a par with such masterpieces as the *Iliad* or the *Chanson de Roland;* it has been the subject of hundreds of research studies by scholars of many countries and has been translated into all the world's principal languages.

After looking round the restored cathedral and the unique 16th-century frescoes, we walk along its covered galleries. Here history speaks to us. The Transfiguration of the Saviour Monastery was visited by Ivan IV, by the Nizhny Novgorod merchant Kozma Minin and Prince Dmitry Pozharsky, who together liberated Moscow from the interventionists in 1612, and by Peter I.

A jetty on the Volga

Monument to the Fighters for the
Revolution. 1958. Sculptor K. Kozlova,
architect M. Yegorenkov

Yaroslavl town centre

132

Cathedral of the Transfiguration of the
Saviour. 1506-16

The Kotorosl River

Detail of a fresco in the Cathedral of the
Transfiguration of the Saviour. 16th c.

We go past the monastery's Holy Gates with their lofty Chasobitnaya (Clock) Tower, walking along well-tended paths and admiring the buildings around us. We come to the museum-preserve. Its rich collection is housed in what used to be the monastery's Seminary and Cell blocks. The exhibition begins with ancient Russian paintings. Among the examples on display are many masterpieces—*The Transfiguration* (1516), *The Smolensk Icon of the Mother of God* (mid-16th c.), *St. John the*

Detail of a wall, the Church of the Epiphany

Church of the Epiphany. 1684-93

Baptist the Winged (16th c.). The Yaroslavl Art Museum also has a fine collection of icons, which would be the glory of any icon collection in the world, such as *The Mother of God of Tolga* (14th. c.). The icon came from the Tolga Monastery beyond the Volga.

When viewing the folk applied art in the museum-preserve, attention should be paid to the rich collection of distaffs. In olden times these were indispensable in town and country household alike. Among the people the work of the spinner was given specially poetic treatment. She was celebrated in songs and ditties. Her image is reflected in the illustrations for broadsides and in toys. Distaffs

Church of St. Elijah the Prophet. 1647-50

were the most prized gifts. They were presented by the father to his daughters, by the bridegroom to his betrothed, and by the husband to his wife. They were decorated with bright colours, intricate carving and presentation inscriptions.

Each department of the History and Architecture Museum-Preserve contains many exhibits that vividly recreate the history of the town. A particularly vivid impression is given of the period during the 17th century when trade, the arts and crafts were at their peak in Yaroslavl. The art and architecture of 17th-century Yaroslavl vastly influenced all of Russia's contemporary artistic trends. The city's advantageous trade and economic position on the intersection of the main Russian trade routes facilitated building on a hitherto unprecedented scale.

Of great interest is the museum's section on the Socialist Revolution, Civil War, and Great Patriotic War of 1941-45. At all the critical moments in their history, the people of Yaroslavl were in the vanguard of the fighters for the freedom and independence of this country. They are rightly proud of their renowned fellow townsmen—Vasily Blyukher, the legendary Civil War hero, and Marshal of the Soviet Union Fyodor Tolbukhin, outstanding military leader in the Great Patriotic War. Very much loved and respected by the citizens of Yaroslavl is the world's first woman-cosmonaut,

Valentina Tereshkova. The museum exhibition tells of the main stages in the development of Soviet cosmonautics and about the life of Tereshkova herself. Also of interest is the museum founded in the village of Nikulskoye, where she was born.

Yaroslavl is a traditional centre of Russian livestock farming. All the world knows the Romanovskaya breed of sheep. Untanned sheepskin jackets have long been made in Russia from the skins of animals bred in the Yaroslavl Region. No less famous is the Yaroslavl breed of the cattle raised in the last century by long-term selection of the most productive local animals.

Gallery in the Church of St. Elijah the Prophet

Harvest. Scene from the life of the Prophet Elisha. Fresco in the Church of St. Elijah the Prophet. 1680-81 ▶

И ЛЕЖАША НА КОЛЕНА МАТЕРИ ДОЇЛⸯ
И УМРЕ.

Yaroslavl butter and cheeses are highly recommended. The craftsmen of Yaroslavl won six of the thirty-three awards at one of the competitions at which the cheese-makers of socialist countries took part. This is also described in the museum exhibition.

After going round the museum, we come out through the gates of the Transfiguration of the Saviour Monastery on to a wide square named in 1920 after Vadim Podbelsky, a revolutionary and a follower of Lenin.

Notice the red Church of the Epiphany, with its five pale-blue domes and graceful bell tower. Going up a little closer, we see that it is richly decorated with glazed tiles. A broad band of tiles graces

Detail of a fresco in the Church of St. Nicholas Nadeyin. 17th c.

the main cube of the building, another runs under the cornice of the covered gallery. Decorative ceramic bands are also to be seen on the drums of the cupolas, and they frame the windows and doors. The red of the walls blends successfully with the green of the tiles, giving the whole structure a cheerful, festive air. This church was built in 1684-93.

The Church of the Epiphany is by no means the only one of Yaroslavl's architectural monuments on which decorative tiles were used. In the 17th and 18th centuries the application of glazed tiles became widespread in the town. Tiles were freely used on the Church of St. John Chrysostom at Korovniki, 1649-54, and on the

Detail of the iconostas in the Church of St. Nicholas Nadeyin. 17th c.

Church of St. Nicholas-on-the-Waters (*Nikola Mokry*), 1665-72, and others. Yaroslavl builders particularly liked to decorate the main altar apse and its central window. The window frames in the Church of St. John Chrysostom at Korovniki are three metres high. Thanks to the golden-green area of the window the entire altar wall is particularly graceful and solemn. The domes of churches in Yaroslavl are also ornamented with coloured tiles. Later the people of Yaroslavl began roofing the church domes with iron. Many of them to this day are still covered with iron tiles in imitation of the old roofs. In our own time, the Yaroslavl Scientific Restoration Studio, using the ancient formulae, has organized the

Metropolitan's Chambers. Late 17th c.
The Museum of Ancient Russian
Painting

The Tolga Icon of the Mother of God.
14th c.

production of coloured tiles which are being used in the restoration of architectural monuments all the way along the Volga.

Like many other ancient towns in Russia, Yaroslavl was once surrounded by mighty walls and towers. It then gradually spread outwards. Suburbs grew up populated with artisans, small tradesmen, coachmen, fishermen. The walls lost their meaning as defence works. Their remains and two watch towers can be seen in the centre of the town. One tower is on the Volzhskaya Embankment; the other, the Znamenskaya, is not far from the *Yaroslavl* Hotel.

On the way from the Epiphany Church to the Znamenskaya Tower you can see the Arcade (*Gostiny Dvor*). It was built in 1813-18 to a design by the architect Pankov. It has been suggested that advice on the project was given by Rossi, the famous designer of many historic buildings in Leningrad. Owing to a fire and repairs in 1911, only the rotunda and part of the north block have survived. But even in this form, the Empire-style ensemble is comparable with the most

outstanding buildings of that period. With the austere beauty of its portico and colonnade, it sets the tone of the street, giving it a particularly ceremonial air.

As you go past the Arcade you will see on your right the tall Znamenskaya Tower—one of the few relics of the 17th-century fortifications. The earth rampart, the 20 stone and timber towers, the deep moat—all these once made the town virtually impregnable. The Znamenskaya Tower was built in 1660-2 on the site of the fire-gutted Vlasyevskaya Tower. A special niche over the entrance archway once contained an icon, *The Sign of the Mother of God,* with the help of which, it was claimed, an epidemic was miraculously averted in 1612, when it could have attacked the volunteer forces of Minin and Pozharsky on their way to liberate Moscow from the interventionists.

Carved and painted distaffs. 19th c.

Detail of a window frame on a peasant house. 19th c.

146

The tower came to be called the Znamenskaya after the icon (*Znameniye* is the Russian word for 'sign').

At the end of the 17th century Russia's tsar and reformer, Peter the Great, ordered samples of the new European-style Russian clothing to be hung next to the 'holy' icon.

Going through the Znamenskaya Tower Gates, we see directly in front of us the *Yaroslavl* Hotel, with a view of the Volkov Theatre in all its splendour on the right.

St. Elijah the Prophet icon. 17th c.

St. John the Baptist fresco. 1694-5. From the Church of St. John the Baptist at Tolchkovo

ст҃го пррка

юаннⷭ҇ прⷣтⷱ

сеⷼапосилаю
агⷢ҇лⷤаⷨⷪⷷ
тⷡⷪⷩⷶⷩⷮⷷ
тⷡⷪⷩⷮⷷⷶⷩⷮⷷ
птⷵⷶⷮⷶⷩⷮⷷ
гⷧ҇ⷶⷣⷱⷩⷫⷮⷷ
тⷶⷩⷶⷩⷮⷷ
ⷠⷶⷩⷮⷷⷶⷩⷮⷷ
гⷩ҇ⷩ

Fyodor Volkov, founder of Russia's first professional theatre open to the general public, was born in 1729 in Kostroma. Volkov received a many-sided education. His interest in the theatre was stimulated by impressions of Russian wedding ceremonies, fairy-tales, folk epics and travelling mummers shows. Visits to the Italian opera and theatre productions in St. Petersburg finally convinced him that it was necessary to found a Russian theatre. And so, returning in 1748, he formed a drama company. In the summer of 1750, he and his colleagues staged a production of Racine's *Esther.* Thanks to Volkov's own talent and to the youth and enthusiasm of the whole company, the show was a hit. They

Frescoes in the gallery of the Church of St. John the Baptist at Tolchkovo. 1694-5

Church of St. John the Baptist at Tolchkovo. 17th c.

subsequently put on Sumarokov's tragedies and plays by Volkov himself on folk themes. And now Russia had its first professional actor, producer-director, and artist (he painted the scenery himself).

The present theatre building was put up in 1911. The acoustics in the auditorium are magnificent and the stage is finished with up-to-date theatrical equipment. There is an interesting museum exhibition in the foyer. For outstanding services in the development of dramatic art the Volkov Theatre was awarded the Order of the Red Banner of Labour on the occasion of its 200th anniversary in 1950. The theatre runs a college that trains artists in the Volkov

151

Altar window in the Church of St. John Chrysostom at Korovniki. Decorated with glazed tiles. 17th c.

Yaroslavl ornamental tile. 17th c.

Ensemble at Korovniki. 17th c. *Left*—the Church of the Mother of God of Vladimir (1669), *right*—the Church of St. John Chrysostom (1649-54)

Theatre tradition.

After looking round the theatre you can dine in the restaurant of the *Yaroslavl* Hotel where you are sure to be offered samples of the local cuisine. After dinner go through the gates of the Znamenskaya Tower once again and stroll down Kirov and Komitetskaya streets. Although they are both small, you will see the Regional Philharmonia, the Puppet Theatre, the Art Fund's Exhibition Hall, Book House, and the *Souvenir* and *Yakhont* shops.

ПЕРВАЯ В МИРЕ ЖЕНЩИНА – КОСМОНАВТ В.В. НИКОЛАЕВА - ТЕРЕШКО

Going from the Znamenskaya Tower along Kirov Street, notice the Church of St. Elijah the Prophet, which is worth a closer look. Built in 1647-50, it embodied the salient features of Yaroslavl 17th-century architecture. The main cube of the church is surrounded by a gallery with chapels and porches; and there is a graceful bell tower nearby. The plan of the church is essentially asymmetrical, but unity of style is preserved, as is the balance of the main architectural masses.

We enter the church through the main porch, which is on the west side, to admire its interior design and decoration. We climb the sloping steps and go into the spacious gallery-parvis. Such covered galleries were a feature of most North Russian churches, whether log-built or of stone. Sheltered from inclement weather, the congregation could discuss matters of general interest.

The carved iconostas inside the church is truly breathtaking. This masterpiece of Russian Baroque was created at the beginning of the 18th century. The gilded vine branches with the clusters of grapes, the flowers and the beautifully proportioned columns and cornices are reminiscent of an enormous and richly worked lace curtain dividing the altar from the main body of the church. The icons date back to an earlier period, the seventies of the 17th century.

When viewing the interior of the Church of St. Elijah the Prophet, be sure to look at the tsar's and patriarch's carved prayer seats. These unusual ecclesiastical thrones were, according to tradition, commissioned in the 1660s for Tsar Alexei Mikhailovich and the Patriarch Nikon (they were originally in the Church of St. Nicholas-on-the-Waters (*Nikola Mokry*). Attention should be paid to one more work of Russian decorative applied art—the carved wooden

The Tereshkova Museum in Yaroslavl's Secondary School No. 32

The Volkov Regional Drama Theatre in Yaroslavl

River Kotorosl embankment

154

Monument to the battle and labour
exploits of the people of Yaroslavl
during the Great Patriotic War of
1941–45. 1968. Sculptor L. Kerbel,
architect G. Zakharov

Trud Square

throne canopy. It is behind the iconostas on the altar and can clearly be seen through the open Tsar Gates. This unique work by 17th-century Yaroslavl woodcarvers is in the form of a tent-roofed church over the throne.

Even so, the chief adornment of the Church of St. Elijah the Prophet are the frescoes. They were painted in the summers of 1680 and 1681 by famous Kostroma artists Gury Nikitin, Sila Savin, 'and their mates'; among them there were also Yaroslavl craftsmen. We are already familiar with the work of Gury Nikitin and Sila Savin from the paintings in the Cathedral of the Trinity of the St. Daniel Monastery in Pereslavl-Zalessky and the Church of the Resurrec-tion in the Rostov Kremlin. These artists also worked on the paintings in the cathedrals and palaces of the Moscow Kremlin, in Kostroma and in other towns. And yet the peak of their work is rightly considered to be the frescoes in the Church of St. Elijah the Prophet. It should be noted that, in spite of their religious subject matter, these frescoes are a unique encyclopaedia of Russian life in the 17th century. They have never been overpainted during the whole three centuries of their existence. They were last cleaned and washed in 1955. Soviet restorers are taking special care of this unique monument of our national culture.

After leaving the church, we go along the Volzhskaya Embank-

New housing estate

Yaroslavl in the morning

Panorama of Yaroslavl

New street

Shopping Centre (*Torgovyie Ryady*).
19th c.

ment. Notice that many houses overlooking the embankment are marked with special preservation boards. This means that they are all under state protection. In Yaroslavl, as everywhere in the USSR, serious attention is paid to the problems of protecting and popularizing our historical and cultural heritage. Great work is being done by schools, technical schools and institutes. For example, a famous historical and architectural monument, the Tolga Monastery, in the part of the city, on the other bank of the Volga, has been under restoration for several years by a special student team.

On the Volzhskaya Embankment, near the steep slope down to the river, where we began our tour of Yaroslavl, there is a monument to the Russian poet Nikolai Nekrasov who dedicated his whole life to the service of the people. He called them to the struggle against their oppressors and believed that the time would come when they would be free.

Nekrasov loved the Yaroslavl countryside. His heart belonged here, and it was here that he found the subjects of his poetry. The Nekrasov Museum-Estate was opened in the Yaroslavl suburb of Karabikha in 1947. When the museum was set up, the atmosphere of the poet's life was reproduced down to the last detail. It was in Karabikha that he wrote *Red-Nosed Frost, Grandfather, Russian Women,* and many fine lyrics. There is

The Nekrasov Museum-Estate

The poet's study

The drawing-room

a big and shady garden round the house in which the poet lived and worked. In the vicinity of Karabikha, Nekrasov, a keen hunter, used to wander with a gun, admire the local scenery and observe the life of the people. It was here that inspiration came to him.

All Soviet people get to know Nekrasov's poetry as children. Typical of the nation-wide love for his creative heritage are the Annual Nekrasov Readings at Karabikha, attended by representatives of all the Soviet republics. The poetry festival in Karabikha is an example of the efflorescence of socialist culture and of the friendship of the peoples. If you have the opportunity, be sure to come to this national festival at Karabikha.

Vladimir

Monuments and places associated with revolutionary and military history

1. Lenin Monument
2. Eternal Flame at the graves of soldiers who gave their lives in the Great Patriotic War of 1941-45
3. Monument in honour of the 850th anniversary of Vladimir
4. Building in which the Headquarters of the Vladimir Military Organization of the RSDLP was accommodated (1906-7)
5. House in which the First Provincial Congress of Soviets was held in October 1917
6. House in which the Vladimir Committee of the RSDLP was accommodated in 1917

Museums

1. The State Vladimir and Suzdal Museum-Preserve of History, Architecture and Art

2. Historical Section of the above museum-preserve
3. Exhibition hall
4. Art Gallery
5. Exhibition of crystal ware, lacquered miniatures and embroidery

Historic architectural monuments

1. Cathedral of the Dormition (1158-60, 1185-9)
2. Golden Gates (1158-64)
3. Cathedral of St. Demetrius (1194-7)
4. The Nativity Monastery ensemble (12th-18th cc.)
5. Cathedral of the Dormition in the Knyaginin (Princess') Convent (15th-16th cc.)
6-12. Architectural monuments (17th-18th cc.)
13. Building of the former provincial administrative offices (1785-90)
14. Shopping Centre (*Torgovyie Ryady*). 1787-90

As you travel round the Golden Ring, you will probably notice that the ancient Russian towns follow one another at intervals of 60-70 kilometres from Moscow, and it is much the same distance from Zagorsk to Pereslavl-Zalessky, from Pereslavl to Rostov Veliky, and from Rostov to Yaroslavl. In this way it would be possible to measure the whole of Russia—to the north as far as Arkhangelsk and to the east as far as Vladimir. One unit of measurement, in the times when these towns were being founded, was the average distance covered in 24 hours by a team of coachmen's horses.

By the old system of measurement the distance from Moscow to Vladimir was three post stages, but by modern standards it is not far—a mere 200 kilometres.

We are crossing the flood plain of the river Klyazma. We shall soon see the suburbs of Vladimir. The scenery round here is beautiful, and by a special decree of the Executive Committee of the Vladimir Soviet of People's Deputies this has been declared a recreational zone. Many people come even from other towns to spend their weekends here.

Ancient Vladimir recently celebrated its 850th anniversary. Before the revolution it was a small provincial town. During the years of Soviet power it rapidly grew into a major industrial and cultural centre. In 1914 there were less than half a thousand workers in the town. Today, Vladimir has over 50 industrial plants producing tractor engines, electric motors, car instruments and programmed lathes. The all-purpose *Vladimirets* tractor has successfully been shown at many international exhibitions. It is bought by dozens of countries. The *Vladimirets* was awarded a Gold Medal and a First-Class Diploma at the Brussels Exhibition.

Education and culture have made tremendous progress here. Vladimir has about a hundred schools, vocational training colleges and technical schools. Thousands of students take courses at Vladimir's institutes. Many have come here from Europe, Asia, Africa and Latin America. The citizens are proud of their phil-

harmonia and drama theatre. The theatre's repertoire is not confined to Russian and Soviet classics, but includes works by Shakespeare, Schiller, Lope de Vega, Molière, and Brecht. Every evening the People's Theatre and universities of culture with faculties of cinema, music and graphic arts open their doors to the public. Over 60 libraries are visited daily by thousands of readers.

As everywhere, the centre of Vladimir is the busiest part of the town. Here are the administrative institutions, big shops, museums and the oldest buildings. It is with them that we begin to learn about the town's history and see the sights.

Vladimir was founded in 1108 by the great Kievan Prince Vladimir Monomakh who gave the town its name. This was the time when the power and might of Kievan Russia were going into a decline, since the land was torn by internecine strife. Monomakh's grandson, Andrei Bogolyubsky, succeeded for a time in subordinating the feudal nobility to the great prince's authority and in creating a strong state nucleus. In 1157 Bogolyubsky transferred the capital from Suzdal to Vladimir. He later organized a campaign against Kiev and took the city, but did not remain there. He ruled South Russia from the banks of the faraway Klyazma. In his efforts to aggrandize Vladimir, he extended it and put up many buildings,

sending for craftsmen and merchants from outside to settle there.

Andrei's brother, Vsevolod III Big Nest, so called because of his numerous progeny, achieved the final recognition of his dynasty as the senior in Russia at the end of the 12th century. Under him, the Vladimir-Suzdal Principality reached its peak. Europe and Asia had to reckon with the 'autocrat' of Vladimir. Bulgars from the Volga, Greeks from Constantinople, merchants from the North Caucasus, from Central Asia and even from the Arab countries, all came to the capital of his principality to trade. The Volga trade route was now almost as important as the Dnieper route 'from the Varangians to the Greeks'.

The city centre

Church in the *posad* (trading quarter outside city wall). 18th c.

Building of the former Nobles' Assembly and boys' high school—a monument of Russian neo-classicism. First half of the 19th c.

The years of internecine strife, raids by nomads and devastating fires have long disappeared. Time has not spared much, but there are still witnesses to the past in the architectural monuments which might be described as the glorious pages of a chronicle in stone.

The most ancient of Vladimir's surviving buildings is the Cathedral of the Dormition. It was begun in 1158 at the same time as the new capital's defence ring, of which only the Golden Gates remain. The chronicle tells us that for this grandiose project craftsmen came from all over the country. Among them were Europeans from the Roman West, allegedly sent to Prince Andrei by the Emperor Frederick Barbarossa; but there were no skilled craftsmen from Kiev. This was no accident, but rather a demonstrative rejection of Kievan assistance and the Kievan artistic tradition. Completed in 1160, the Dormition Cathedral rivalled Kiev's St. Sophia in mon-

The Golden Gates. 1158-64

The arched span in the Golden Gates

umentality and elegance.

The importance of this cathedral in Russia's history is shown by the fact that, beginning with Yury Dolgoruky's son Mikhalka, all the Vladimir and Moscow princes ascended the throne there, including such powerful Russian military leaders and statesmen as Alexander Nevsky, Dmitry Donskoi and Ivan III. Up to the end of the first quarter of the 14th century the cathedral was the most important church in Russia.

The Cathedral of the Dormition has come down to our own times with extensions. In 1185 the cathedral was badly damaged by fire, and in 1185-9 it was surrounded with mighty walls and was thus boxed, as it were, inside the new building. Four more domes were mounted on the corners, making a total of five. Describing the building work of that period, the chronicler wrote with pride that this time there was no need to fetch craftsmen from abroad.

From the very beginning the cathedral was rightly considered an architectural masterpiece and well worthy of imitation. The Cathedral of the Dormition in the Moscow Kremlin was built at the end of the 15th century by the Italian architect Aristotle Fioravanti who modelled it on the cathedral in Vladimir. As a treasure of the Russian and world art, it has now been taken under the protection of the state. Work done by Soviet restorers inside the cathedral has disclosed fragments of unique frescoes from several periods—1161, 1189, the 13th century, and authentic work by Andrei Rublev, Russia's painter of genius who, with Daniil Cherny and others, worked on the cathedral interior in 1408, painting the frescoes and icons.

Most of the surviving Rublev frescoes are under the choir and depict *The Last Judgement*. Rublev's images are impressive for

their intense humanity and depth of characterization. In the faces of the saints and believers, which suggest the faces of ordinary Russian people, the artist has embodied the moral ideal of spiritual purity, humility, and yet at the same time a rare strength and determination. Andrei Rublev's icons for the iconostas in the Cathedral of the Dormition are now preserved in the Leningrad Russian Museum and in the Tretyakov Gallery.

Another world-famous painting that was once in the Cathedral of the Dormition is *The Vladimir Icon of the Mother of God.* This work of genius by a Byzantine master is now in the Tretyakov Gallery.

Cathedral of the Dormition. 1158-60

Old Vladimir observation platform—the Museum of Town Life in the 19th century

In the grounds of the ancient Kremlin founded by Vladimir Monomakh are two of the city's most remarkable monuments. We have already seen one of them, the Cathedral of the Dormition. As we go a little closer to the limestone Cathedral of St. Demetrius (1194-7), we notice that the dome on the high drum is topped with a golden 'helmet'.

The helmet-shaped covering of the domes is one sign of ancient architecture up to and including the 16th century. In the 17th century 'onion' domes had already become widespread in Russia. Seen from a distance, they suggested lit candles held up to the sky. Later, in the 18th century, during the spread of the Baroque style, the appearance of the domes changed. The 'onion' domes became two-staged, fantastically girdled round the upper part. If you remember this small detail, you will find it easy in future, as you get to know the monuments, to determine roughly to what period they belonged.

The Cathedral of St. Demetrius was part of the prince's palace complex. It is one of the most perfect specimens of work by the Vladimir-Suzdal architects. Built during the years of North-East

The Last Judgement. Detail of a fresco in the Cathedral of the Dormition. 1408. By Andrei Rublev

Bell tower, the Cathedral of the Dormition. 19th c.

Russia's power and prosperity, solemn, calm, richly decorated with bas-reliefs, it seems to personify the power and wealth of the Vladimir Principality. Together with the columns of the blind arcade, each of which ends in a sculpture, there are over 1,300 bas-reliefs on the cathedral walls. All three portals and the cathedral drum, with its narrow slit-shaped windows, are cunningly decorated with carvings. Even the five corner columns are in the form of animal claws digging into the ground.

Stone carvings on the Cathedral of St. Demetrius

The Cathedral of St. Demetrius. 1194-7

The Cathedral of St. Demetrius was built with blocks of white limestone. Since, at the time, this soft, easily worked stone was the main building material for churches and princes' palaces, all the Vladimir-Suzdal architecture of the 12th-13th centuries is known as whitestone. By the time the cathedral was built, the local craftsmen had many such structures to their credit. Working with white stone, the architects and master stonemasons accumulated valuable experience. They could build high walls and steep vaults with ease.

No less skilfully did the Vladimir builders handle stone when decorating it with reliefs which were undoubtedly carved by local craftsmen. In style, the stone 'pat-

terns' of the Cathedral of St. Demetrius are a unique blend incorporating heathen Slavonic interpolations with their roots going back to folk carving in wood, and elements of Byzantine, Roman and even proto-Renaissance art. And yet the carved decorations and the architectural image of the cathedral as a whole are national in spirit, techniques, methods, and plasticity.

After viewing the Cathedral of St. Demetrius, note the 18th-19th-century civic buildings in the ancient centre of Vladimir. Between the Cathedral of St. Demetrius and the Cathedral of the Dormition are the former offices (*Prisutstvennyie Mesta*), an 18th-century administrative building in the Russian neo-classical style. Particularly beautiful are its side façades, decorated with columns of the Corinthian order. Not far from the monument in honour of the 850th anniversary of Vladimir stands the building of the former Nobles' Assembly (*Dvoryanskoye Sobraniye*), 1826. It bears marked traces of the enthusiasm among the architects at that time for ancient Greek culture and art. Directly adjoining the building of the Nobles' Assembly is another Russian neo-classical monument—the former boys' high school. It is decorated with an eight-columned Doric portico that gives the whole structure a ceremonial appearance.

After viewing the Russian neo-classical monuments we come out

The Lunacharsky Regional Drama Theatre

on to Moscow Street, the town's main thoroughfare, and at its far end we see the famous Golden Gates.

The Golden Gates of Vladimir were built in 1158-64 and, like the Golden Gates of Kiev, were the main entrance way to the town. They were called golden because the massive oak leaves were originally covered with gilded sheet copper. As you look round the monuments in Vladimir, you cannot possibly miss the Golden Gates. Their well-proportioned mass can be seen from a distance. On the way you can go shopping for souvenirs, books on Russian and Soviet art, and guidebooks.

The Golden Gates were the main defence bastion of the west part of the town and also served as a triumphal arch. The conquerors of the Teutonic Knights in the famous Battle on Ice on Lake Chudskoye passed through these gates in 1242. The victorious troops returning from the Battle of Kulikovo marched through them in 1380. After Napoleon's invasion of Russia in 1812 it was from those gates that detachments of the Vladimir People's Militia left on the long march to take part in the historic Battle of Borodino near Moscow.

The Golden Gates were surmounted with a gilt-domed church, round which there was a battle platform reached by a staircase leading into the five-metre-thick south wall.

View from the theatre foyer

Today the Golden Gates house a military historical museum exhibition and a gallery of heroes of the Soviet Union who were natives of the Vladimir Region. The heroes' portraits, documents and personal belongings are on display. A portrait of Nikolai Kamanin is there, he was one of the first awarded the Order of Lenin and the Gold Star for his part in the rescue of the Chelyuskin Expedition in 1934. Kamanin was an active participant in the Great Patriotic War. In the post-war years he became the first head of the Cosmonauts' Training Centre. Under his guidance Yury Gagarin trained for and carried out his flight in 1961.

As in any ancient Russian town, the new is cheek by jowl with the old in Vladimir. Near the Golden Gates, in the red brick building of the former town church, there is a museum exhibition of works by contemporary artists: caskets by miniaturists, embroidery from the world-famous village of Mstyora in the Vladimir Region, articles by the glassblowers of Gus Khrustalny, and jewellery.

The distant past can be seen in the ramparts, all that remains of the 12th-century defence works. They can still be viewed from the south side of the Golden Gates. Near the rampart, on the premises of the former fire observation tower, a Museum of Ancient Town Life was recently opened. Take a look round: you will find much to interest you there.

The *Traktir* Restaurant

On the city's main street

Building of the Literature and Music
departments of the Teacher Training
Institute

Construction work in progress

Our route takes us from the Golden Gates back to the centre. On the way, we recommend you to have a look at the drama theatre, named after A. Lunacharsky, the first People's Commissar for Education. The theatre bills will give you some idea of the company's range. The theatre has successfully toured Moscow, Leningrad and many other big cities. If you have time, visit the Taneyev Concert Hall. The distinguished Russian composer, Sergei Taneyev, was a native of Vladimir. A fine teacher, he raised a whole galaxy of brilliant musicians, including Sergei Prokofiev and Dmitry Shostakovich—two great 20th-century composers.

In the centre of Vladimir, near the obelisk commemorating the 850th anniversary of the town, is the local Regional Studies Museum in which the past of the Vladimir land is interestingly illustrated by a wealth of archaeological material. Conspicuous among the exhibits are unique 12th-century fabrics, the whitestone tomb of Alexander Nevsky, and the personal belongings of the military commander Dmitry Pozharsky.

Here, too, in the town centre, is the complex of the Knyaginin (Princess's) Convent near the remains of the north-west ramparts. It was founded at the turn of the 12th century by the wife of Vsevolod III, hence the monastery's name. Its main church was the Cathedral of the Dormition. The present cathedral building was put up at the end of the 15th and beginning of the 16th centuries on the ruins of the ancient church. In the first half of the 17th century, when the convent was at its most prosperous, the Cathedral of the

Bogolyubovo. The prince's residence, founded in the 12th c.

Dormition was decorated (1647-8) by an artel of 'the sovereign's icon-painters' under Mark Matveyev. Two centuries later the frescoes were redone, and the former pictures were buried under the new paint. For many years Soviet restorers, architects and painters worked to bring back its original appearance to this unique relic. Their efforts were entirely successful, and the wall paintings in the Cathedral of the Dormition—the most important monument of Russian monumental painting in the first half of the 17th century—can be seen by the visitor in all their original beauty.

The creative work of the restorers is absorbing, interesting and extremely difficult. Physics, chemistry and modern technology come to their aid in our times. The fine precision work of the restorer is like that of the surgeon. Incidentally, the restorer often uses the same tool—a scalpel. True, the operation done by the restorer sometimes takes months, as is convincingly shown at the exhibition by a series of photographs, the 'history of a disease', taken at various stages during the restoration process.

Vladimir is impressive for the variety and number of its museums.

The Sungir Archaeological Museum was opened recently on the east fringe of the town. Sungir, the northernmost settlement in Europe of the Upper Palaeolithic

Period (Stone Age), was discovered by archaeologists in 1957. The site of the excavations has been declared a protected zone, and the Sungir Museum-Pavilion has been built there. It is a low building of brick and bright concrete. Four metres below are the main exhibits: a geological cross-section of the spot has been reproduced with traces of the various epochs and cultures.

The Sungir Museum is not far from Bogolyubovo. Once the country residence of the Vladimir princes, this is now a favourite beauty spot for the townsfolk and for tourists.

Prince Andrei Bogolyubsky's Palace was built in 1158-65. By this, the prince gained control over

Bogolyubovo. Cathedral of the Dormition. 19th c.

Bogolyubovo. Detail of the wall, the Cathedral of the Nativity. 12th c.

'Holy Canopy'. 17th c.

the estuary of the Nerl which flows into the Klyazma, and over the whole waterway to the Volga on the territory of the principality. The palace was surrounded with limestone walls. Inside were the prince's chambers, the Cathedral of the Nativity and various service buildings.

The surviving towers and the passage leading to the prince's chambers are a unique example of ancient Russian architecture. Time has changed them considerably. The staircase tower, square in plan, together with the passage and the cathedral, have subsided almost two metres into the ground. A remarkable triple window with two columns has been preserved on the upper platform of the staircase

Church of the Intercession on the Nerl. 1165

Details of the architectural decoration on the Church of the Intercession on the Nerl

tower; it gives a wonderful view of the Nerl and its water-meadows.

The exterior of the staircase tower and the passage are decorated with bands of light arches and columns blending with the arcade frieze of the Cathedral of the Nativity which was rebuilt in the mid-18th century. The mighty ramparts, raised eight centuries ago, revive for us the bygone majesty of this prince's town of Bogolyubovo.

A kilometre away from Bogolyubovo, reflected in the tranquil and clear waters left by the river Klyazma, are white walls and the dome of a solitary church. This is the Church of the Intercession on the Nerl (1165). It is famous for its ideal proportions and the soft outlines of the whitestone carvings. The church stands on a man-made hill. In ancient times this was paved with white stone and had a drainage system. The church foundations are exceptionally deep (530 centimetres).

The façades of the Church of the Intercession are vertically divided into three parts. Approximately half-way up, there is a blind arcade on graceful columns resting on console-masks carved in limestone. The wall decorations are interesting for the various figures of animals and human beings. Interesting, too, is the composition, with the beasts savaging one another: this expresses in allegorical form the need for a united Russia.

Our tour of Vladimir ends with a view of the Church of the Intercession on the Nerl. We can rest in the comfortable *Vladimir* Hotel with its *Beriozka* Shop and a restaurant serving Russian dishes. Refreshed in the morning, we can continue our journey round the Golden Ring. Our next stop will be Suzdal.

Suzdal

Monuments and places associated with the history of the revolution

1. Building used for the underground press of the Suzdal group of the RSDLP (1905-7)
2. Building in which Soviet power was proclaimed in the town (22 November 1917)

Museums

1. Branch of the State Vladimir and Suzdal Museum-Preserve (the Kremlin: 1—Cathedral of the Nativity, 13th-16th cc; 2—Archbishop's Chambers, 15th-18th cc.; 4—Church of the Dormition, 1713; 3, 5, 6—monuments of ecclesiastical architecture, 18th c.; 7—ramparts of the Kremlin, 12th c.;
2. Museum of Wooden Architecture and Peasant Life. 18th-early 20th cc. 8—wooden Church of the Transfiguration, 1582-94;

9—wooden Church of the Resurrection, 1776

3. Museum of Folk Art of the RSFSR 10—Saviour Monastery of St. Euthymius, 16th-19th cc.

Historic architectural monuments

11. Shopping Centre (*Torgovyie Ryady*), 1806-11
12. Church of the Resurrection (1720)
13. Church of the Emperor Constantine (1707)
14. Ramparts of the *posad* (trading quarters), 13th c.
15. Church of the Sign (1749)
16. Church of the Deposition of the Robe (1777)
17. Civic building (18th c.)
18. Church of St. Nicholas (18th c.)
19. Intercession Convent (16th-18th cc.)
20-34. Monuments of ecclesiastical architecture (16th-19th cc.)
35. Church of the Archangel Michael (early 18th c.)
36. Church of SS Flor and Lavr (1803)

The road from Vladimir to Suzdal runs through open fields. There is arable land wherever you look. This is the ancient granary of the Vladimir lands that accounted for their populousness and wealth. Half-way along the route lies the big village of Borisovskoye. For a thousand years the land here was tilled by the descendants of the first farmers. They are tilling it to this day, but on big mechanized, multi-branch collective and state farms and now the life of the village people differs little from that of the city folk.

The road takes us on and on, and then suddenly, in the distance, from the top of Poklonnaya Hill, we can see Suzdal spread out before us, one of the richest treasures of Russian national culture. Our first view is a vague silhouette, spiky with many belfries and churches which now vanish from sight, now reappear as the road climbs upwards again.

Suzdal is situated on the river Kamenka which falls into the river Nerl a few kilometres away. In olden days this land was known as the Suzdal *opolye*. Settlers were attracted by the rich, fertile land, suitable for agriculture. The first written reference to Suzdal occurs in the chronicle in the entry for the year 1024 and mentions one of the earliest peasant uprisings in the history of Russia.

Initially, in the 11th century, Suzdal was the name given to several small settlements situated quite close to one another. The increasing external danger, together with the peasant uprisings, made it necessary for the feudal lords and rich people to build fortifications. A rampart and a stockade were put up round the central settlement. In 1096 Suzdal was mentioned in the chronicle as a 'town'. The central fortified part was formed by the Suzdal Kremlin whose ramparts have remained in excellent condition to this day. This is where our tour begins.

We go down the street which runs across the old fortress's well-preserved east moat, 30-35 metres wide, and the rampart that surrounded the fortress. In the 18th century, the top of the rampart was levelled and made into a boulevard.

Its slopes, covered with centuries-old trees, are up to 17 metres from the bottom of the moat; the total perimeter is 1,400 metres. A gap in the road indicates the spot where once stood the fortress's main entrance tower, the log-built Ilyinsky Gates, to which ran the wooden walls along the top of the rampart. The south-west Dmitrovsky Gates of the Kremlin led to the ancient St. Demetrius Monastery over the river, while the south-east, or Nikolsky Gates led to a bridge across the Kamenka.

On the right, directly behind the rampart, stands the little Church of the Dormition. It was put up in 1650 on the site of an older, log-built church. Rebuilt in 1713, it is one of Suzdal's most

Protected Suzdal

Festival bazaar

The town centre

Shopping Centre ((*Torgovyie Ryady*). 19th c.

View over the Suzdal Kremlin

198

graceful and typical monuments.

It is not known exactly when the whole fortress was built but it must have been at the beginning of the 12th century, since that was when Vladimir Monomakh raised the first stone building here—the brick Cathedral of the Dormition of the Mother of God and the adjacent prince's courtyard. The cathedral quickly fell into decay and was demolished. In 1222-5, a new whitestone building went up in its place.

Excavations at the foot of the south wall of the present cathedral have brought to light some fascinating remains of the Monomakh's first building. The original cathedral was built of fine brick, or 'plinfa'. A fragment of the fres-

Panorama of Suzdal

coes also survived on the lower part of the wall. However, the new cathedral did not remain intact either. In 1445 the upper part collapsed. By 1530 the top of the cathedral had been rebuilt with brick and had acquired the five domes characteristic of those times.

After the Cathedral of the Dormition in Vladimir, it is clear from the external form of the Suzdal Kremlin's central Cathedral of the Nativity that this is a building of the same type. It is a large city cathedral considerably lengthened by extensions to the altar part. There have been additions to the main entrances on three sides, thus giving the cathedral its cruciform plan. It is built of irregular slabs of porous tufa. Only the architectural details are of white stone and they stand out in contrast with the soft, uneven background of the wall.

The architects combined the Vladimir style, refined and detailed decorative finish, with a simple, rough texture of wall surface reminiscent of the Novgorod churches. Flatness of ornamentation predominates in the carvings. In aiming for a decorative effect on the façades, the builders tried to free themselves from the influence of the structure.

Attention should be paid to the west, and, in particular, the south, or Korsunsky Gates of the Cathedral of the Nativity. They are an extremely rare example of Russian 13th-century applied art. The

gates are covered with an exquisite pattern which was engraved on copper sheets etched with acid and then gilded. The cathedral gates testify to the technical skill and superior artistic standards of the ancient Russian craftsmen.

Inside, fragments of 13th-century frescoes have been preserved, and also fragments of wall paintings dating back to 1635. Particularly beautiful are the paintings in the princess's burial vault (near the west wall), with a luxuriant maroon-red flower in the centre.

The octagonal stone tent-shaped bell tower was built in the 1630s, a few dozen metres from the cathedral, to which it is not directly joined.

The central Kremlin ensemble

201

Cathedral of the Nativity. 13th-16th cc.

Carved portal capitals, the Cathedral of the Nativity. 13th c.

is completed by the Archbishop's Chambers, an architectural complex which grew up during the 15th-18th centuries. As research has shown, the oldest part is in the south-east corner—the Archbishop's Chambers, dating back to the end of the 15th century. A private church with a Refectory was built in 1559 to the west of the chambers. At the end of the 17th and beginning of the 18th century the old buildings were incorporated into the new and more spacious Archbishop's Chambers.

Detail of a fresco in the Cathedral of the Nativity. 1233

The west Golden Gates, the Cathedral of the Nativity. 1230-3

The main block of the chambers, whose façade overlooks the cathedral courtyard, is closely connected with the cathedral. The main entrance to the chambers is on the axis of the cathedral's west portal. From here, two ceremonial staircases lead into the spacious hall. The visitor walks through to find himself in the vast uncolumned hall of the Krestovaya (Cross-vaulted) Chamber. Then comes a series of rooms used for various purposes.

A magnificent monument of civic architecture, the Archbishop's Chambers were neglected for a long time. Now, after restoration, they have become a museum with an extremely rare collection. The exhibition gives the visitor a detailed picture of the social, economic, and political history of Suzdal, its architecture and the various stages of restoration work in the town. In the Ancient Russian Art Section of the museum there are rare examples of casting, chasing, engraving, and ivory carving. In the development of the jeweller's art, 15th-century Suzdal was on a par with such important Russian art centres as Novgorod, Moscow and Tver. No less famous were the works of the Suzdal embroideresses. Invaluable examples (16th-17th cc.) of 'painting with the needle'—the shrouds, palls, *pelena* cloths, covers for vessels, and robes for the clergy represented in the exhibition were done for the most part by nuns. The coloured fabrics, embroidery with pearls,

The Archbishop's Chambers. 15th-18th cc.

Bell tower, the Cathedral of the Nativity.
1635-36

Entrance to the Archbishop's Chambers
Museum

precious stones, gold, and silver delight the visitor, especially the connoisseur of this rare craft. The Suzdal specimens of portrait embroidery are not inferior to the masterpieces of the Moscow Kremlin and Hermitage museums.

The pride of the museum is a collection of old icons. Inheriting and developing further the Byzantine and Kievan traditions and drawing on the experience of the Novgorod artists, the 13th-century Suzdal craftsmen created their own local school. In the 14th-15th centuries, what came to be called the Vladimir-Suzdal school of ancient Russian painting reached its pinnacle. The best works of this period are notable for elegance,

lyrical outline, soft colouring, unity of tone and, most important of all, inspiration. It was these qualities of Suzdal painting that were subsequently adopted as a basis by the Moscow school which emerged in the 14th century.

Both the Tretyakov Gallery and the Leningrad Russian Museum have in their collections many first-class works by Suzdal painters. In the exhibitions of these museums icons by Suzdal artists are exhibited side by side with the works of the other schools. Here, in Suzdal, the visitor has the opportunity to trace the development of the local school from the very best examples. Particularly worthy of mention are three 15th-century icons in the Krestovaya Chamber:

The Apostle Peter. Christ. The Apostle Paul—three icons from the deesis. 16th c.

Krestovaya Chamber—the columnless hall in the Archbishop's Chambers. Late 17th c.

208

The Museum of Wooden Architecture and Peasant Life

Top left, Church of St. Nicholas from the village of Glotovo. 1766

Top right, Carved decorations on a wooden house. 19th c.

Bottom right, Church of the Transfiguration from the village of Kozlyatyevo. 1756

the icon *The Mother of God with Child,* known as *The Eleusa* (14th century), *St. Nicholas* (14th century), *The Shroud* (15th century) and *The Family Trees* (16th century).

In the museum and its branch, the Church of the Resurrection-on-the-Market-Place (*Voskreseniye-na-Torgu*), there is an exceptionally beautiful collection of coloured wooden sculptures, tools, and architectural decorations—window frames, bargeboards, carvings of scenes from everyday life, and other remarkable work by Suzdal artists.

Virtually a continuation of the exhibition in the Church of the Resurrection is a wooden township which has grown up in recent years near the Kremlin on the far side of the river Kamenka on Dmitriyevskaya Hill. Log-built churches, huts, barns, drying sheds and mills have been brought here from various hamlets and villages in the Vladimir Region. What inexhaustible creative imagination went into all these structures! The people showed wisdom and skill in their use of wood, that most rewarding and favourite building material of olden times. Using the simplest of tools—the axe, the chisel and the plane—Russian people created uniquely beautiful buildings without the use of nails or iron. The creations of the folk architects displayed in the Suzdal museum are notable for talent, skill and industry.

It looks remarkably appropriate, this log-built township amid the stone architecture of Suzdal. For almost a quarter of a millennium, beginning in 1238, not a single stone building of importance went up here. However, as far as can be judged from the extremely rare references in manuscript books and other documents, those two and a half centuries were the period

Windmills and barn. 19th c.

Panorama of the Museum of Wooden Architecture

when Suzdal wooden architecture flourished. Unfortunately, none of it has survived to our own times. Churches, dwelling houses and various functional and administrative buildings were made of wood. The examples of wooden architecture brought in from various parts of the Vladimir Region recreate this remarkable feature of Suzdal in bygone days.

To see the other sights of the town, go back to the central square, where stand the beautiful churches of the Resurrection (1720) and of Our Lady of Kazan (1739). The first is particularly interesting; the architectural forms are especially typical of Suzdal in the first half of the 18th century. It is a large whitewashed brick cube with a

pyramidal roof crowned with an
onion-shaped dome on a tall drum.
The one and only low, but very
wide, apse (the semicircular pro-
jecting part of the building) is
joined to the church at the east end.
Next to the Church of the Resurrection stands its bell tower, for
which magnificent coloured tiles
were used.

Between the Church of the Resurrection and the river, on the
very edge of a steep cliff overlooking the Kamenka, is the Shopping
Centre (*Torgovyie Ryady*), an interesting example of Russian neo-
classical architecture. The booths
and shops of the *Torgovyie Ryady*
are at the service of the customer
to this day. Here, on the river bank,
we see the Church of the Entry

Church of SS Boris and Gleb. 1747

Church of St. Nicholas. 1720-39

Fortress walls and towers of the Saviour ▶
Monastery of St. Euthymius. 16th-17th cc.

into Jerusalem (1707) and the Church of St. Parasceva Pyatnitsa (1772).

Opposite, on the north-east side of the square, are two more interesting architectural monuments: the Church of the Mother of God of Compassion, with its typical Suzdal bell tower and tent roof with slightly concave sides (1787), and the Church of the Emperor Constantine (1707) with a small rotunda in the neo-classical style subsequently added to the west façade.

The Church of the Emperor Constantine, with its south façade looking on to the square, is elegant and monumental. Like an embroidered border on the smooth white wall, there is a wide cornice of

The Refectory of the Church of the Dormition. 1525

small, deep-cut horseshoe-shaped motifs and a band of skittle-like ornaments and baluster-shaped tiles. Contrasting with the graceful simplicity of the wall, five slender and highly ornate domes rise over the roof. These shaped summits create an atmosphere of festivity and emphasize the church's importance in the square as a whole. A bell tower helps the Church of the Emperor Constantine to blend with its 'subordinate', the Church of the Mother of God of Compassion, into a complete composition.

Liberally adorned with different coloured domes on their tall drums, the church buildings all over Suzdal give the town a magic of its own. The tent roofs of the many bell towers are slightly concave

Monument to Dmitry Pozharsky by the walls of the Saviour Monastery of St. Euthymius. Sculptor Z. Azgur

The Archimandrite's house. 16th-17th cc.

and richly decorated—another architectural feature typical of Suzdal. All this blends organically with the old dwelling houses which are not to be demolished but are being improved and carefully restored.

In adapting Suzdal to the needs of the present times, the planners are thinking well ahead. It has been decided not to put up new buildings in the old part of the town. And if this should be unavoidable in certain cases, special designs must be used, with the height of a typical old building as a limiting factor. Only under these conditions will it be possible to preserve the uniqueness of an architectural ensemble that has taken centuries to form.

The architects planned and are successfully carrying out new housing projects outside the old part of Suzdal, but here, too, with a view to the local landscape. A housing estate has grown up on the outskirts with well-appointed houses, a kindergarten-cum-nursery to accommodate 140 infants, a school for 1,200 children, a shopping centre and public catering establishments.

Our route runs from Sovietskaya Square in the centre along Lenin Street, the town's main thoroughfare, to an impressive historical and architectural complex, the Saviour Monastery of St. Euthymius (Spaso-Yevfimiyevsky). There are several sights to be seen on the way. There is, for

House in the *posad* (trading quarter outside city wall). 17th c.

Ancient domestic utensils

instance, the imposing sixty-metre-high bell tower of the Deposition of the Robe (Rizopolozhensky) Monastery. It was put up in the Russian neo-classical style of the first half of the 19th century. The bell tower dominates the whole of Suzdal. The monastery's cathedral, built in 1560, is also worthy of attention. But the true gem of the Deposition of the Robe Monastery is the famous Holy Gates (1688) flanked by the two octagonal tent-roofed towers decorated with pilasters and coloured glazed tiles—the work of Suzdal builders Mamin, Shmakov and Gryaznov.

The Saviour Monastery of St. Euthymius is the biggest architectural ensemble in Suzdal. Situated on the high bank of the Kamenka,

it dominates the landscape beyond the river. The high stone walls, over a kilometre long, with twelve mighty towers, give the monastery the outlines of a formidable citadel which, indeed, is exactly what it was for centuries. The walls are 7.5 to 8.5 metres high and over 6 metres thick. All along the walls there are battlements and loopholes which once ensured the all-round defence of this monastery-fortress.

The most interesting of the towers is the Vkhodnaya (Entrance), situated on the south side. Now the entrance to the museum in the Saviour Monastery of St. Euthymius, the tower is 23 metres high, and because of this it was used as a watch tower. The smooth

Gornitsa (room in peasant's hut)

Bell tower of the Deposition of the Robe
Monastery. 19th c.

The Holy Gates of the Deposition of the
Robe Monastery. 17th c.

Church of St. Parasceva Pyatnitsa (1772)
and the Church of the Entry into
Jerusalem (1707)

walls over the low archway are so richly ornamented that they resemble lacework in stone.

The Vkhodnaya Tower adjoins the 17th-century Church of the Annunciation-over-the-Gates. It is decorated with shaped window frames and a sumptuous cornice. After going through the church, we find ourselves inside the monastery. Here is the centrepiece of the composition—the Transfiguration of the Saviour Cathedral (1594) whose walls were painted with frescoes in the 17th century.

Of special interest is the monastery bell cote, which combines elements of the 16th and 17th centuries. In the 16th century the bell cote was in the form of a column, but when it became necessary to increase the number of bells, a gallery was added to it with three arches on top.

Of the other monastery buildings, notice should be taken of the 16th-century Refectory Church of the Dormition added to the Chambers of the Archimandrite whose private church it was. The first storey of the building of the Brothers' Cells (17th century) is impressive. It is now a unique museum of contemporary folk art. Sculptors, painters, potters, embroideresses, glassblowers and tinsmiths from all over Russia are represented here by their best work.

In the 18th-century Prison Block the atmosphere of confinement has been reproduced. The prison in the Saviour Monastery of

St. Alexander of the Neva Monastery.
17th c.

Detail of the Church of SS Boris and
Gleb at Kideksha. 1152

Architectural ensemble at Kideksha.
12th-18th cc.

224

St. Euthymius was founded on the orders of Catherine II in 1766. It was used to lock up freethinkers and insurgents—the enemies of the church and the autocracy. One of the cells was earmarked for Leo Tolstoy who was excommunicated by the church and who was to have been sent here.

When you come out of the Saviour Monastery of St. Euthymius, be sure to go to the viewing platform nearby. From here, on the high, steep bank of the Kamenka, you can see one more remarkable Suzdal ensemble as if it were on the palm of your hand—the Intercession Convent, founded in 1364.

It would be possible to say much more about Suzdal, but it

Main Tourist Complex

Souvenirs shop

Motel

is best for visitors to see for themselves.

After coming to Suzdal and breathing the atmosphere of the genuine Russian past, do not be in a hurry to leave the town. Visit one of its comfortable restaurants. You can dine at the *Trapeznaya* (Refectory) where you can try the ancient monastic cooking. If you happen to be in Suzdal during winter, you can visit the cosy and cheerful *Pogrebok* (Cellar). For lovers of comfort in the modern style we recommend the restaurant of the Main Tourist Complex.

The problems of tourism and the provision of the necessary facilities are being worked on by Suzdal's Scientific Research and Design Institute, the head organization for the conversion of the town into a model international tourist centre. In 1978 the designers and specialists who have been working out and implementing the plans were awarded the USSR State Prize for Architecture and Construction. In 1983 the town of Suzdal received the Golden Apple Prize from the International Federation of Journalists and Writers.

A new housing estate has grown up in a picturesque bend of the river Kamenka not far from the former Intercession Convent. The architects call it the Main Tourist Complex. It has been incorporated into the landscape with a view to the rhythms, shapes, volumes and salient features of the 16th-18th-century monastery buildings.

Everything necessary is already there: an up-to-date hotel to accommodate 430, with a cinema-cum-concert-hall for 500, a restaurant seating 500, a swimming-pool

and a complex of motels for 300 guests, together with a car-servicing station.

The book of comments on Suzdal's facilities is full of grateful entries in many languages. Not far from the Main Tourist Complex, a small but very comfortable hotel is being fitted out in the Intercession Convent. Many tourists will certainly enjoy staying in the log-built houses which are to be put up in the convent grounds. There will also be a restaurant, a café and a concert hall.

The glory of Suzdal, heir to the Kiev of the great princes, 'mother of the Russian cities', the centre of all North-East Russia, is long past. The town is now a quiet district centre in the Vladimir Region. Even so, it is widely known at home and abroad as a protected town-museum, rightfully considered the shrine and pride of the nation.

The history of restoration work in Suzdal goes back to the first years of Soviet power. This noble cause has been served by such outstanding restorers and scientists as A. Varganov, G. Vagner, and Lenin Prize winner N. Voronin. It is thanks to the generous concern of the Soviet state and the dedicated work of the scientists and their assistants that Suzdal has become a unique laboratory for the most advanced methods in the restoration and preservation of architectural monuments and will never lose its enchanting beauty.

Ivanovo

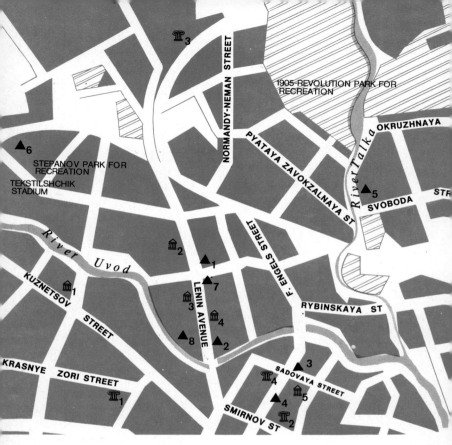

Monuments and memorable places associated with revolutionary history

1. Lenin Monument
2. Mikhail Frunze Monument
3. Fyodor Afanasyev Monument
4. Memorial complex *To the Fighters for the Revolution*
5. Memorial complex *Red Talka*
6. Building used in 1906 for the underground press of the Ivanovo-Voznesensk organization of the RSDLP
7. Building in which Soviet power was proclaimed on 25 October 1917
8. Building used for the Headquarters of the Red Guards (1917-18)

 Museums

1. Museum-study of Mikhail Frunze
2. Exhibition Hall
3. Art Museum
4. State Museum of History and Art

5. House-museum of the Ivanovo-Voznesensk City Soviet of Workers' Deputies (the first of its kind in Russia)

 Historic architectural monuments

1. "House of the Collective"—living accommodation for 400 workers' families (1931)
2. Shudrovskaya Chapel (17th c.)
3. Wooden church (17th c.)
4. Complex of Higher Educational Establishments—architectural monument (1927-32)

A big industrial and regional centre, Ivanovo is an integral part of the Golden Ring. It is linked by rail and road with Moscow, Yaroslavl, and Vladimir, and is easily accessible from any point on the Golden Ring.

Compared with the other towns we have visited, Ivanovo is young: in 1971, it celebrated its centenary. But the village of Ivanovo, which eventually grew up into a town, has been known for a long time. The first reference in writing goes back to 1561. By the mid-17th century this large trading and industrial village was already known abroad for its products. Linen from Ivanovo was eagerly bought by English agents. The local printed fabrics were very much in demand on the home market. Production began to develop at the end of the 18th century. Ivanovo calico is world famous to this day. In our own times large consignments of fabrics from the Ivanovo textile complexes are exported to many foreign countries.

Ivanovo is of considerable historical importance for its services to the Soviet Union: it was the town of the first Soviets. They came into being at the will of the Russian proletariat in Ivanovo-Voznesensk during the 1905 Revolution.

The Ivanovo textile workers had much experience of strikes as a weapon of struggle. As early as on 22 December 1897, 14,000 Ivanovo-Voznesensk workers declared a strike. The reasons for the proletariat's action were the appalling working conditions, the low wages, the cruelty of the owners and, in particular, the reduced number of holidays. Among the strike leaders were members of the Ivanovo-Voznesensk Union of Workers which maintained contact with the Moscow Union of Struggle for Liberation of the Working Class. Soon, the Union or Workers became the Ivanovo-Voznesensk Committee of the Russian Social-Democratic Labour Party (RSDLP). The workers were out on strike for three weeks. Army units were deployed against them. But, in spite of these repressive measures, the strikers won certain concessions from the owners.

The 1905 strike (12 May to 23 July) was directed by the Bol-

Detail of the monument *To the Fighters
for the Revolution*. 1975. Sculptor
D. Ryabichev, architect Ye. Kutyrev,
artist M. Malyutin

*Revolutionary Demonstration
by the Workers in 1905* Diorama.
By Ye. Deshalyt

Here, in October 1917, Soviet power was
proclaimed in the town

This house was used in 1905 for secret
meetings by the battle detachment of
the Ivanovo-Voznesensk RSDLP
organization

shevik organization of the RSDLP headed by Mikhail Frunze, subsequently to be an outstanding government and political figure in the Soviet state and a major military leader in the Civil War. The strike began as an economic one, but soon became political. On 15 May, the workers created the Assembly of Plenipotentiaries—virtually Russia's first town Soviet of Workers' Deputies. The Soviet functioned as an organ of revolutionary power: it independently authorized freedom of meetings, of speech, and of the press, established revolutionary order in the town and adopted measures to give assistance to strikers and their families. The tsarist authorities sent out troops against the strikers. On 3 June 1905, by the river Talka, people at a workers' meeting were shot down. The general strike lasted 72 days. Only starvation compelled the workers to accept partial concessions from the owners and to go back to work.

The revolutionary events of 1905 in Ivanovo-Voznesensk have been immortalized in a number of monuments and memorials. In Rev-

Red Talka Memorial. 1975. Sculptor
L. Mikhailyonok; architects
V. Vasilkovsky and Ye. Kasatkin

Monument to Mikhail Frunze. 1957.
Sculptor Yu. Neroda; architect
A. Rostkovsky

olution Square, in the town centre where our tour begins, stands a monument *To the Fighters for the Revolution*—a bronze sculptured group on a granite pedestal: a worker is snatching a red flag—the symbol of struggle—from a comrade who has been hit by one of the executioners' bullets.

The greatest shrine of the Ivanovo townspeople is the memorial on the river Talka, where the idea of a Workers' Soviet was born and where the tsarist butchers shot down the striking proletarians of Ivanovo-Voznesensk at a meeting. The memory of the heroes of the revolutionary struggle is honoured in the town. There is a monument to Mikhail Frunze. Soviet sculptor Yury Neroda and

House-Museum of the First Soviet
(the building is no more extant)

architect Anatoly Rostkovsky have created a vivid image of this military leader who came from the people. One of the textile mills is called *Krasnaya Talka*. Working-class leaders, Olga Varentsova and Fyodor Afanasyev, are commemorated by monuments and by the names of Ivanovo factories.

Ivanovo, the capital of this textile world, is a rapidly developing town. The latest equipment has been installed at the blended yarn and worsted complexes, at the *Bolshaya Ivanovskaya Manufaktura* Complex and at the *Vosmoye Marta* Textile Works. New factories and powerful industrial plants in Ivanovo are producing machines for textile mills and peat processing, also autocranes, bor-

Ivanovo today

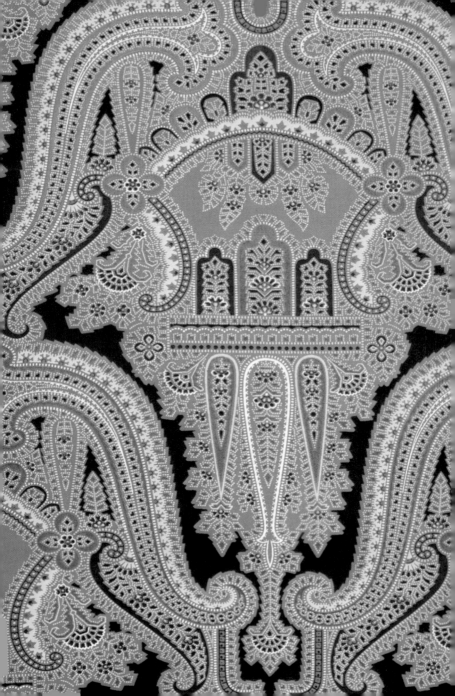

ing lathes and testing instruments.

Ivanovo is a town of new building projects. Housing estates began to go up in the first years of Soviet power. The workers in pre-revolutionary Ivanovo-Voznesensk lived in slums and in the gloomy, sordid 'doss-houses', as they were called. In the 20s and 30s the leading Soviet architects carried out a number of building projects. In 1927 one of the founders of world constructivism, Victor Vesnin, built the State Bank in Ivanovo. Academician Ivan Fomin designed the beautiful Institute of Chemistry and Technology. In the 30s Alexander Vlasov—builder of such famous structures in Moscow as Krymsky Bridge, the Gorky Recreation Park, and the sports complex at Luzhniki—put up the Bolshoi Drama Theatre, an imposing building in the classical style.

Today's construction projects are impressive in their scope and size. New housing estates, palaces of culture and sport, public libraries, and hospital complexes are opened every year in this organically developing contemporary town with its half a million inhabi-

Old fabrics and printing blocks—exhibits in the Ivanovo Museum of Regional Studies

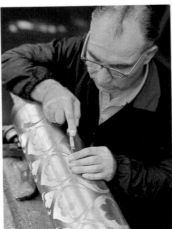

tants. Local tours will give you the chance to become more closely acquainted with the monuments to the history of the revolution and with the countless new building projects.

In spite of its industrial profile, Ivanovo is an artists' town. It is enough to think of the vivid, colourful products of the Ivanovo textile factories—the countless varieties of patterned cottons and colour combinations—to realize that dozens of inspired artists had a hand in their making. They are carrying on in the old traditions of folk decorative art. In the Ivanovo-Voznesensk Museum of Regional Studies you will see where the skill of the contemporary artists originated. Examples of old printing blocks in the museum exhibition testify to the fine taste and truly folk character of the Ivanovo printed fabrics.

The whole of the Ivanovo Region is rich in art traditions. Take, for instance, Palekh, the 'village-academy' of folk art. It is the next stop on our journey.

There is a beautiful church in the centre of the big and handsome

village of Palekh. The inscription on the outside of the west wall has preserved the builder's name: *Master Yegor Dubov.* The church was built in the austere ancient Russian style. In contrast with the whiteness of the exterior, the interior is strikingly colourful. The 17th-century Church of the Exaltation of the Holy Cross is a branch of the Museum of Palekh Art. The upraised iconostas in the Russian Baroque style was executed by local craftsmen. The icons painted in Palekh were done in the tradition of Russian 15th-17th-century painting. In the iconostas of the south

Birth of a printing pattern

244

chapel the 16th-century carved Tsar Gates are of particular value: they came to the church from the ancient town of Uglich on the Volga.

In the pleasant two-storey Museum of Palekh Art the work of this famous village is fully represented in the form it adopted after the Great October Socialist Revolution.

Palekh miniatures are a form of folk painting in tempera on lacquered papier-mâché articles—an art form which draws on its own traditions and has its own style, techniques and methods. Everything about it is out-of-the-ordinary: the special paints, the colours, the rhythms, the outlines, the use of gold, the sometimes fantastic forms of vegetation, architecture and ornamentation; the imagination and fantasy, the outstanding skill and, at the same time, the keen sense of reality and of the present.

The village of Palekh

Interior of the Cathedral of the Exaltation of the Holy Cross. 17th c.

With the development of capitalism in the 19th century, the once integral skill of the Palekh craftsmen broke up into a series of separate operations, and the artist became a sort of factory hand exploited by owners who earned millions from the toil of the icon-painters dependent on them.

The October Socialist Revolution opened the way to inspired creative work. The art of Soviet Palekh is inseparable from the Socialist Revolution. A great friend of the Palekh craftsmen was Soviet writer Maxim Gorky who saw their work as one of the little miracles being worked by the Revolution, evidence of awakening creative powers in the masses of the working people, one of the most significant leaps from the 'necessity' of forced labour to 'free creativeness'.

Palekh icon painting had one noteworthy feature: it preserved the lustre of ancient Russian art and its great schools of painting in Novgorod, Yaroslavl and Moscow. For this reason old Palekh was much valued by the archaeologists, experts and connoisseurs. The

founders of contemporary Palekh art drew on this tradition that was deeply rooted in the art of the people; they gave it a new lease of life.

What has contemporary Palekh art inherited from ancient Russian painting? First, the material and the method; second, the system of decorative and graphic forms, such as 'hills', 'palaces', 'grasses' and the like; third, style—that is, certain techniques of drawing and painting, the use of gold paint, and original means of composition connected with a distinctive method of depicting space on a flat surface.

At the same time, this art has many new features, new elements and forms which, combining with the traditional elements, substantially change and modify them. In Soviet times, for instance, the Palekh artists have completely prevailed over the mediaeval ascetic manner of portraying man as a fleshless, refined creature with a dark face and no live physical colouring. The landscape has changed, as have the architecture and the ornamentation, to say nothing of the subjects and the ideological message of this art.

Palekh art is the people's art because it was created as the result of the amateur activity of simple peasant craftsmen; because it has always developed further the living elements of ancient Russian painting and folk crafts; because this art form is only

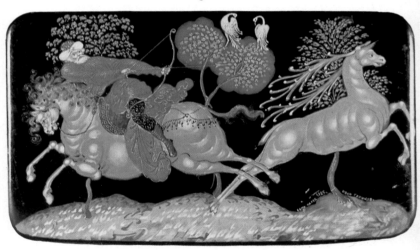

The Reindeer Hunt. By I. Golikov. 1925

Troika. By I. Golikov. 1925

possible in connection with the whole mass of the Russian people's skill—their songs, traditions, fairy-tales and folk epics; finally, because in an unusual form it reflects the social life and spiritual world of Soviet people today.

Ivan Golikov, the founder of Soviet Palekh art, was a man of outstanding natural talent. He was the first to apply egg yolk tempera

to papier-mâché, to paint stage scenery and execute paintings on a monumental scale.

Golikov imagined the revolution as a violent whirlwind. "I've painted many battles because I've taken part in fighting myself and, having seen cavalry clashes and engagements, cities on fire, looting, the horror of refugees, children and old people, I painted it all," explained Golikov. He often painted a battle with a city on fire in the background: the huge vortex of flames blazing and soaring against the black setting of the sky; leaping horsemen with slashing blades, rearing horses, often red or yellow in colour so that they are like the play of the untameable element of fire.

Long Live the Red Army! By D. Butorin. 1926

Prince Igor Taken Prisoner. By R. Belousov. 1964

On the Stream. By B. Yermolayev. 1973

Reapers. By I. Markichev. 1933

Song of Stepan Razin. By N. Golikov. 1970

Apart from battles, Golikov also favoured highly expressive subjects such as hunts, strolls, *troikas* and folk dances.

Golikov's masterpieces can be seen in the display cases of the Museum of Palekh Art. Another memorial is the modest little timber house in which he lived and worked. Golikov's house vividly demonstrates that it is not special colours and brushes, but a special spirit inspired with imagination, that is the main source of imperishable art. Ivan Golikov was not alone. His example was an inspiration to other Palekh artists who had been icon-painters. An artel of ancient painting was formed in 1923. It included masters of the lacquered miniature, such as Alex- ander Kotukhin, Ivan Vakurov, Ivan Bakanov, Ivan Markichev, Ivan Zubkov, Alexei Vatagin, Aristarkh Dydykin, Nikolai Zinovyev and Dmitry Butorin. Together with Golikov, they are rightly considered the founders of contemporary Palekh art. Their work is the pride of the museum, and their names are on the marble memorial plaques to be seen on many of the modest houses in Palekh. It is fascinating to go for a walk round a village in which every house is a home of art.

We had good reason for calling Palekh a 'village-academy'. The rudiments of the craft have been, and are being, passed on to the young by the experienced masters. The art college is much

251

In the village of Palekh

'Twas at Our Gates. By Ye. Grosberg.
1976

Near Palekh

Lace patterns in wood

House-Museum of the Artist Pavel Korin

loved and cared for by the people of Palekh, and it now has a new and beautifully equipped building. This is where the future artists are trained.

Over a hundred and fifty skilled artists work for the Palekh Art Production Studios, and many of them are members of the Artists' Union of the USSR. Palekh keeps its creative standards at a high level, and its lacquered miniatures are in demand all over the world.

Tourists in the ancient village are hospitably welcomed at a restaurant specially built to cope with the large numbers of visitors. Even there you can see Palekh interior decorations worthy of any museum.

Palekh is getting younger. The Master Plan for the development of the village envisages a new building for the Museum of Palekh Art, new studios for the miniaturists, a House of Culture, libraries and other facilities. The historic centre of Palekh with its characteristic atmosphere and landscape will become a protected zone.

Palekh is away from the railways. This famous village is linked with Moscow by bus service. Your route will take you through the fields and forests of the Russian Non-Black-Earth Zone, a poetic landscape that has given the world a charming art, a land undergoing rapid growth and development in every way.

The *Palekh* Restaurant

Dear reader,

If you have been studying
this book at home, we hope
it has made you want to visit
the Soviet Union and
especially to go for a trip
around the Golden Ring of
ancient Russian towns. We
welcome you from the bottom
of our hearts.
But if this book has travelled
with you on such a journey,
we still prefer to say *au revoir*
but not good-bye.
Do come and see us again!
You may be sure of a warm
welcome.

77+7А6.1
П41

По «Золотому кольцу» России
Фотопутеводитель
(на английском языке)

Авторы текста и составители Юрий Александрович Бычков,
Владимир Александрович Десятников
Специальная фотосъемка Вадима Петровича Тужикова
В издании использованы фотографии Л. Вейсмана,
В. Гиппенрейтера, В. Дорожинского, Ю. Меснянкина,
Л. Раскина, Е. Рябова
Перевод Александра Миллера

Зав. редакцией Т. В. Гуськова
Редактор Н. А. Красновская
Редактор перевода Т. Е. Туркина
Художественный редактор Т. С. Богданова
Технический редактор А. И. Быковская

ИБ № 1314
Сдано в набор 22.02.89. Подписано в печать 09.06.89. Изд. № 11/3-8971.
Формат 84×108/32. Бумага мелованная. Гарнитура таймс. Печать офсет. Усл. печ. л.
13,44. Усл. кр.-отт. 85,26. Уч.-изд. л. 16,280. Тираж 35 000 экз. Заказ 126. Цена 5 р. 90 к.
Издательство «Планета», Москва, 103031, ул. Петровка, 8/11
Ордена Трудового Красного Знамени Калининский полиграфический комбинат
Государственного комитета СССР по делам издательств, полиграфии и книжной
торговли. 170024, г. Калинин, пр. Ленина, 5.

 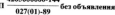

П $\dfrac{4205000000\text{-}144}{027(01)\text{-}89}$ без объявления